A Connected Curriculum
for Higher Education

Dilly Fung

Foreword: Energising an Institution

It is customary, in a Foreword, to begin by sketching a large context in which the book in question might be comprehended and then perhaps to pick out one or two of its key features and end by affirming the value of the book in front of the reader. On this occasion, I shall reverse this order. Let me start, therefore, by asserting that *A Connected Curriculum for Higher Education* is both a splendid book and, for all those who care about higher education and universities, a crucially important book.

That assertion actually contains a number of suggestions on my part. One is that this book offers important insights separately for higher education and for universities, that is to say both for students and their learning on the one hand and for universities as organisations on the other hand. Every page is packed with insights and practical suggestions for advancing students' learning and their wider experience: that is immediately evident. Furthermore, in the Connected Curriculum idea, there are the makings of a coherent vision and plan of action for institutional transformation.

At the centre of the Connected Curriculum idea lies the hope and, indeed, the demonstration that it is possible, within universities, to improve the relationship between teaching and research. In a sense, of course, this thought should never have needed to be uttered. For 200 years, since the modern idea of the university was born at the end of the eighteenth and beginning of the nineteenth centuries, it has been taken for granted in many quarters that a distinguishing feature of universities is that they be institutions that not only are spaces of both teaching and research but also that those two functions are intimately intertwined. However, for the past three decades or so, huge forces (national and global) have tended to pull research and teaching apart; and so the matter of their relationship has become a matter of wide concern.

It might be tempting to address this matter in a rather limited way, looking at the actual relationships between research and teaching – which, characteristically, may be expected to vary even within the same university – and focusing on a particular aspect, in trying to bring the two activities closer to each other. (The question has to be asked: just why should the Pro-Vice-Chancellors for Teaching and for Research ever talk to each other? After all, in many universities, their roles have become quite separate.) A huge virtue of *A Connected Curriculum for Higher Education* is, to the contrary, that it sees, in this issue of the relationship between teaching and research, the profound and much wider matter as to what it is actually to be a university. This book, therefore, contains – albeit subtly – a vision for the university in the twenty-first century.

Connectedness lies at the heart of this vision. There are no less than twelve dimensions of connectedness that can be glimpsed here, namely connections:

1) Between disciplines
2) Between the academy and the wider world
3) Between research and teaching
4) Between theory and practice
5) Between the student and teacher/lecturer/professor
6) Between the student in her/his interior being – and in his/her being in the wider world
7) Between the student and other students
8) Between the student and her/his disciplines – that is, being authentically and intimately connected epistemologically and ontologically
9) Between the various components of the curriculum
10) Between the student's own multiple understandings of and perspectives on the world
11) Between different areas – or components – of the complex organisation that constitutes the university
12) Between different aspects of the wider society, especially those associated with society's learning processes.

We could legitimately say that here is a vision of a well-tuned learning project, working at once on the personal, institutional and societal levels. Even if only some of these envisaged forms of interconnectedness bear fruit, we are surely in sight of a heightened *institutional vibrancy*, with new institutional energies being released as the various components of the extraordinary complex that constitutes a university exhibit new connections. With research and teaching, with disciplines, and with student and tutor and student and student, engaging with each other in new ways, there will doubtless occur a *satisfactory frisson*, as the entities of a university make contact anew. There is a newly energised university on the cards here.

That is surely ambitious enough. But I detect in this book an even greater ambition. It is none other than to realise the potential of the university in the twenty-first century. Do we not detect here a university in which its component parts not just listen to each other and pay heed to each other but also bring the university into a new configuration with the wider world in all its manifestations? There is surely a sense here of the university coming out of itself to attend to all the many ecosystems in which it is implicated – the economy certainly, but the ecosystems too of knowledge, social institutions, persons, learning, the natural environment and even culture. The Connected Curriculum opens, in short, to a new idea of the university, a university that is fully ecological, attending carefully to the many ecosystems in its midst.

This idea of the university – lurking here in the Connected Curriculum – is none other than a sense of the possibilities of and for the whole university. It is a bold idea of the university as such. Within it lies a sense of the university as having responsibilities towards its ecological hinterland, towards its students, knowledge (and the disciplines), learning, the economy and the wider society. In a century doubtless of much turmoil and challenge, the university is not in a position to save the world (whatever that might mean) but it is in a position to play a modest part in helping to strengthen the various ecosystems of the world. The idea of the Connected Curriculum holds out that hope.

This will not be an easy project to bring off. The kinds of change being opened here will be provocative in the best sense, stretching academics, students, and institutional leaders and universities themselves into challenging and even difficult places. But there are, in this book, numerous examples and vignettes that testify to the practical possibilities ahead. There are, too, and crucially important, the words of individuals involved that offer immediate testimony to the enthusiasm that this kind of project, when carefully orchestrated, can engender. And there are helpful questions that will aid examination both of self and of institutional practices. This is a living project and an energising project. I cannot think of a more important initiative for higher education and the future of the university.

Ronald Barnett, Emeritus Professor of Higher Education,
Institute of Education, London

Acknowledgements

I am deeply grateful to the many people who have helped me to develop the ideas expressed in this book. The monograph could not have been written without the numerous and diverse colleagues and students from across UCL, from many disciplines, whose expertise, creativity and humanity are a constant source of inspiration. The Connected Curriculum concept could not have been enhanced and applied to practice in so many contexts without the wholehearted backing of UCL President and Provost Professor Michael Arthur and of Vice Provost Professor Anthony Smith, whose leadership and personal support have been so empowering. Special thanks are also due to my excellent colleagues in the UCL Arena Centre for Research-based Education (formerly the Centre for Advancing Learning and Teaching), for generously sharing their academic and professional expertise and their friendship, and also to many UCL colleagues from across the academic disciplines and professional teams, including Dr Karen Barnard, Dr Fiona Strawbridge, Carl Gombrich and Professor John Mitchell, for their encouragement and valuable contributions.

I am indebted to the scholars from around the world who contributed a 'vignette of practice' to this monograph, to help illustrate the ways in which the ideas in the book can play out in different contexts. Additional illustrations in the text have been drawn from many more colleagues working for universities and organisations across the UK, Europe and beyond with whom I've been able to explore the concept of the Connected Curriculum through talks, meetings and collaborative events.

Special thanks are due to Professor Ron Barnett for his warm support for the Connected Curriculum expressed through the Foreword; to Professor Mick Healey for his valuable contributions to the Connected Curriculum initiative as UCL Visiting Professor; and to Professors Angela Brew, Philippa Levy and Carl Wieman for their very helpful correspondences in relation to this monograph. I am grateful, too, to Vice

Provost Professor Simone Buitendijk (Imperial College) and Dr Claire Gordon (London School of Economics) and to my former colleagues at the University of Exeter for their inspiration and personal support.

Most of all, I'm grateful to my wonderful family – Peter, Ruth, Jos, Paul, Lucy and Michael – for their love, insights and good-humoured encouragement, and to every one of my former students, over more than three decades. All of you have shown me why it is so important to commit to creating societies in which bridges are more appealing than walls.

Contents

List of figures

List of tables

ntroduction

; it possible to bring university research and student education into closer, more symbiotic relationship? In doing this, can we create etter spaces for critical dialogue within and across disciplines? And can uilding on the relationship between research and education become catalyst for making better connections between academics, students nd 'real world' communities? This book argues that it is not only ossible but also potentially transformational to set out to do these hings. Introducing a new, values-based Connected Curriculum frame-'ork for developing these ideas and related practices, it opens windows nto a spectrum of possibilities for institutions, departments, faculty lembers and students in higher education.

The Connected Curriculum framework is represented graphically 1 terms of a core principle and six associated dimensions (Chapter 1). he core principle, or underlying premise, is that students at all levels f the curriculum can benefit in multiple ways by engaging actively in :search and enquiry. Students can also contribute to the impact of the istitution's research, and engage local and wider communities directly 'ith the findings of their investigations.

The framework thus builds on the classic Humboldtian notion of le unity of teaching and research, breaking down unnecessary divi-ons between the practices of research and student education. It also romotes the value of rich dialogue and collaboration among diverse articipants in higher education, and of interactions between universi-es and wider communities.

In pedagogic terms, the emphasis is on research-based education Chapter 2); that is, education in which structured opportunities are cre-ed for students to learn through research and active enquiry at every vel of the curriculum. There is growing evidence that students bene-from engaging in collaborative and dialogic enquiry, whereby each dividual's prior assumptions are challenged through interaction with hers as well as with the object of study.

1

The six associated dimensions of the Connected Curriculum framework are considered in turn (Chapters 3–8). Throughout, the focus is on empowering faculty members and students to take a fresh look at the shape of the whole taught programme, whether undergraduate or postgraduate, to see whether the student journey has the right balance between, on the one hand, structured learning activities and, on the other, spaces for individuals to make choices and even to take risks. There is no set recommendation for the ways in which modules or units of study combine into a whole programme leading to a higher education award, but each chapter shines a light on aspects of this challenge. Where and how will students build understandings of what it means to know in the discipline, of how this discipline connects to others, and of how the edges of knowledge can always be extended through research?

However, the Connected Curriculum approach is not just about promoting a particular pedagogy or a range of possible curriculum structures, as useful as these might be. It is not even just about creating better links between a department's research and its programmes of study, although this is a repeated motif. At its core it is about shining a light on knowledge itself, and on the goals and values underpinning the interconnected missions of education and research. Across higher education, scholars are investigating the world through different lenses. Their focus may be, for example, on observing and analysing the physical world, on interpreting the human world, or on advancing professional practice. Creating a curriculum that links these diverse landscapes of enquiry more explicitly and more creatively for students has the potential not only to enhance the quality of education but to enrich research itself, and to strengthen further the impact research and scholarship already make on the world.

The argument of the book is not just theoretical. University College London (UCL), a large research-intensive university in the UK, has adopted the Connected Curriculum framework, and it has become an integral part of its published education strategy for 2016–21 (UCL 2016a). Chapters 3–8 include examples, from UCL and also from the wider higher education sector, of how these ideas can become a reality in different disciplinary, institutional and national contexts, and Chapter 9 provides a 'case study' overview of how the framework is opening up new developments and possibilities in its home institution.

Chapter 10 concludes by reviewing the dimensions of the framework, presenting a series of questions and two contrasting graduates' stories to provoke discussion in departments. It then considers possible barriers to change for institutions and how these might be overcome so that the synergies between education and research can be more fully realised, benefiting both students and wider society.

Introducing a shared 'framework' for thinking about how curriculum is designed, and how students can become partners in both research and educational development, may be considered to be a risky business. Are academic freedom and diversity of practice not threatened? The higher education sector is, after all, full of 'quick fix' initiatives, which can remove agency from faculty members and professional colleagues. The Connected Curriculum is emphatically not designed to be a short-term fashion. It is not about ticking boxes or adopting the latest jargon. On the contrary, it is about promoting spaces for genuine critical dialogue, within and across existing research groups and teaching departments, in which the very concerns that scholars, professional staff and students have about agency and opportunity can be addressed. The intention is not to narrow down thinking about curriculum but to open it up; not to create more uniformities but to set practice free to become more diverse.

A Connected Curriculum for Higher Education offers practical suggestions, illustrated by examples of current practice in the sector, for connecting students more closely with research, within and across disciplines. More fundamentally, it argues that if diverse students are empowered to collaborate actively in research and enquiry at every level of the curriculum, engaging others with their ideas and findings, both education and research will be able to contribute more effectively to the global common good.

1
Introducing the Connected Curriculum framework

We are now at a watershed in higher education.
We are faced with the need for great change, and we have
the yet unrealized opportunities for achieving great change.
Nobel Laureate Carl Wieman (2016b)

1 The Connected Curriculum framework: an overview

What is the Connected Curriculum framework? It is a simple graphical schema (Figure 1.1), designed to be a catalyst for:

- sharing excellent practices already taking place in higher education institutions, and
- stimulating new creative ideas for enriching the curriculum and the wider student experience.

Represented at the centre of the model is the underpinning pedagogic orientation of the Connected Curriculum approach, that of learning through research and enquiry. The contention is that the predominant – although not necessarily exclusive – mode of learning for students should be active enquiry *and*, where possible, engagement with current research that is pushing forward what is known in a particular field. As knowledge does not confine itself to disciplinary boundaries, however, that enquiry should push across traditional subject borders to create new analyses and connections. This core principle will be examined later in this chapter.

Surrounding the core are six associated dimensions of practice, each highlighting the need for connectivity in a particular area. These

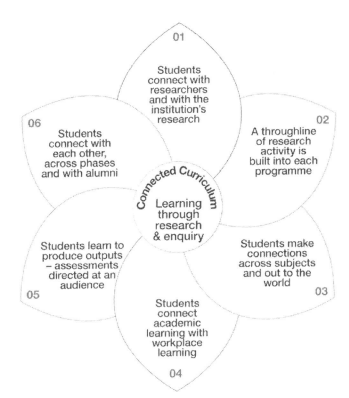

Fig. 1.1   The Connected Curriculum framework

values-based dimensions are introduced briefly here, before each is explored in greater depth in subsequent chapters.

The six dimensions of the framework: an overview

1. Students connect with researchers and with the institution's research

This dimension focuses on the importance of explicitly inviting students to connect with researchers and research as an integral part of their learning journey. Students ideally need regular opportunities to learn about their institution's research, as well as other research relevant to their studies. They may, for example, become affiliated to research groups, or investigate the work of one researcher in depth. Through engaging with 'real world' research studies, students can be encouraged to start to formulate their own research questions, and empowered to explore and critique what might be described as the edge of knowledge in their discipline(s) of study (Chapter 3).

2. A throughline of research activity is built into each programme

Each programme of study needs to be designed in such a way that students experience a connected sequence of learning activities that empower them, step by step, to apply the skills and dispositions needed to undertake investigations. The right balance is needed between compulsory and optional modules (or units of study), so that students can make critical, creative connections between apparently disparate elements of their learning. The pattern of assessment and feedback activities across the whole programme, both formative and summative, plays a key part here. Overall, the assessment and feedback activities should encourage students to link different aspects of their learning, for example by requiring them to draw on different themes and skills within a final capstone module or by asking them to work towards a curated Showcase Portfolio (see Chapters 4 and 7).

3. Students make connections across subjects and out to the world

This dimension focuses on the importance of students making conceptual connections between their own subjects and other disciplines. At appropriate points in the programme of study, they should ideally be able to step outside their home discipline(s), for example by studying with students and scholars from outside their main subject field. Not only can students encounter a range of different ways of investigating the world, they can be equipped to engage with some of the complex challenges of modern society, including its systemic inequalities. Students benefit from engaging with international perspectives on their disciplines and from developing an awareness of knowledge traditions from cultures that differ from their own. Through connecting across disciplines and out to the world, students can be empowered to articulate their own values and consider their current and future contributions to society (Chapter 5).

4. Students connect academic learning with workplace learning

Students need to be able to connect academic learning explicitly with the areas of knowledge, skills and approaches needed both for professional work and for lifelong learning. Their programme of study, as a whole, should equip students for life and work in a world in which technological innovations are the norm, and in which social and organisational needs change rapidly. Students also need to become increasingly *aware* that they are developing a rich range of understandings, skills, values and attributes to take with them into their professional lives, and be able to articulate these effectively. They can also be empowered to engage in critical dialogue with others about the evidence-based application of knowledge to society (Chapter 6).

5. Students learn to produce outputs – assessments directed at an audience

Through some of the work they produce for the purpose of being assessed by faculty members, students can engage explicitly with external audiences. Some of their assessments can become, in effect, 'outputs' from their research and enquiry, which mirror those produced by researchers. The work that students produce should vary in form across the programme, enabling them to develop the digital practices and communication skills needed to engage with diverse audiences. Ideally, some of their work will even be developed in partnership with local or wider communities – whether in person or online – and make a meaningful contribution to society (Chapter 7).

6. Students connect with each other, across phases and with alumni

Taught programmes and co-curricular opportunities should enable diverse students to connect with one another, both in their year group and across phases of study. This can be cultivated, for example, through designing collaborative assessment tasks and by putting on departmental events. Postgraduate research students can have structured opportunities to engage with students on taught programmes, for example by delivering seminars on their emerging work. Peer mentoring can be offered and alumni invited to get involved as inspirational partners and advisers. The focus for this final dimension is on ensuring that students feel a sense of belonging as they study and of being part of an inspirational learning and research community. The key is to work in partnership with students and alumni to make this happen in ways that are authentic and sustainable (Chapter 8).

2 The purpose of the framework

The Connected Curriculum framework aims to open up areas of dialogue among faculty members, students, professional staff and others and to cultivate new possibilities for practice. It is designed to stimulate discussion about important relationships – between research and education, between diverse people and their different knowledge horizons, and between academia and wider communities.

The initiative is underpinned by the notion that education is relational: not just in the sense that we need to engage in dialogue to learn as we study and/or research but that the purpose of education itself is to create societies in which dialogue, respect for others and openness to new ideas are promoted. It is *not* therefore the intention that the framework closes down possibilities but that it leads to creative, original ideas for new directions of travel.

The six dimensions of the Connected Curriculum build on a commitment to the integration of education and research for the benefit of all. The focus is not just on the 'effective' learning of individuals, but also on higher education as a values-based, research-education ecosystem that needs to be developed as a connected whole. The dimensions are underpinned by a conception of education as a 'common good', as a collective social endeavour characterised by 'shared responsibility and commitment to solidarity' (UNESCO 2015, 78). Do the educational opportunities we offer reaffirm the collective dimension of education: the sense that education is a shared social endeavour? And in what ways do educational practices draw on and even influence the work of researchers?

Building on philosophical underpinnings, the Connected Curriculum framing elicits a series of important questions about the nature of higher education. These questions are considered here, before we turn to practical applications in each of the following chapters.

3 Universities in a changing world

In the context of a changing global landscape and the development of new technologies, universities have complex challenges. As multi-faceted and multi-layered organisations, they need on the one hand to achieve cultural and economic sustainability and on the other to maintain focus on multiple objectives. The volume and impact of an institution's research remain, in many areas of the world, key criteria for success. Yet in the UK and internationally universities are educating increasing numbers of people; they are therefore seeking to develop an institutional ecosystem which enables them to provide excellent education for students *and* high-quality research. How can this best be done?

When addressing this challenge, fundamental questions arise. What are universities *for* now? Those of us who work in universities could ignore this question and choose to focus simply on quick, instrumental initiatives designed to solve immediate problems – to improve student satisfaction rates, for example, or to improve operational efficiency. But decision-making can surely be set much more productively within the context of exploring fundamental values and purposes. As Barnett (2016) puts it, we need to consider our possibilities afresh and examine what it is to be an 'authentic' university in the twenty-first century. Within the complex and interconnected ecology of political, social, economic and cultural imperatives and practices, what do we want our university, our department, our research and our taught programmes of study to *be*?

In a diverse educational sector, with very diverse participants from many nations and backgrounds, to speak of shared values at all may itself seem challenging. Those with a stake in higher education include potential and current students, their families and communities, and all the organisations (including charities, community groups, corporations, professional bodies, funding bodies and governments) that benefit from citizens' education. So the range of people who have a stake in higher education is vast. Perhaps values in relation to the purpose of higher education are not and cannot be shared?

Certainly there are perceived tensions within universities between those who see education predominantly in terms of training for the benefit of economic success, whether that of the individual or society, and those who conceive of education as being a more rounded set of cultural practices which are fundamentally about human development and 'becoming', human relations, and the development of a 'good' society. A parallel set of tensions is associated with research: should it always be directed at *doing* – at solving problems, and making a demonstrable impact on the world – or is research to be seen less instrumentally, as pushing the boundaries of what it is possible to know and think?

These tensions relating to the purposes, policies and practices of higher institutions are well documented in the academic literature produced *by* universities: the higher education sector draws on many of its disciplines to engage critically with its own characteristics and practices as a sector, producing nuanced arguments. It can be difficult for participants within higher education – leaders, faculty members, professional staff and students – to see the wood for the trees in this debate. Equally, external stakeholders – including governments, funding bodies, employers and parents – may find it hard to work out what the higher education sector, with its different mission groups, is trying to achieve.

The Connected Curriculum framework creates a lens, shapes a window, through which the higher education community can look afresh at its own possibilities. It allows a light to shine on the strange, customary separation of education from research in the strategies and practices of institutions. It is very common for institutional mission statements and strategies to treat the various strands of their activity as if they were separate. Research and student education (or 'learning and teaching') are the most prominent of these strands; other related areas include widening participation, knowledge exchange, enterprise, global and public engagement and lifelong learning. But these all spring from and/or contribute to education and research as the two core activities. Building on the synergies between all of these areas is no mean feat and the rise of the so-called audit culture in recent years has arguably made it more difficult than ever (Blackmore, Blackwell and Edmondsen 2016). We will briefly consider issues relating to the audit culture, before examining the theoretical framing and underpinning values of the multidimensional Connected Curriculum framework.

4 Audit cultures: tensions and opportunities

An issue of key importance to universities in many parts of the sector internationally is that of assuring the quality of their provision. The notion of quality management is pervasive and quality judgements are made regularly both internally and externally, leading to the ranking of institutions in league tables. In the UK, a Teaching Excellence Framework (TEF) (QAA 2016b) has been introduced, with the declared aim of incentivising universities to 'devote as much attention to the quality of teaching as fee-paying students and prospective employers have a right to expect' (BIS/Johnson 2015).

The TEF mirrors the UK's now-established Research Excellence Framework (REF), which ranks the quality and strength of research produced by individual scholars, their disciplines and their institutions. These quality review cycles in the UK are echoed in many parts of the world, forming a repeated motif in the life-rhythms of scholars and institutions.

It is easy to highlight the problems with such an audit culture in both education and research, and this has been done extensively in academic literature (see, for example, Morley 2003; Apple 2005). Certainly there is evidence that quality reviews can be expensive and time-consuming, and that they may sometimes have perverse consequences. Even in an era of learning analytics and big data, the things that we can reliably evaluate through 'metrics', for example the number of times students attend class or access a virtual learning environment, we may see as less important than the deeper impact of education on individuals and communities. The latter needs more nuanced, qualitative expressions and judgements. The introduction into English and Welsh universities of student fees, which have seen significant increases in a short time and which are set to rise again with the introduction of the Teaching Excellence Framework, has added to the spotlight on quality in the UK. Will student 'customers' be happy with what they have purchased? And will situating students *as* customers adversely affect the educational and research culture? These are all legitimate questions for analysis.

However, the notion that there need be no accountability for the quality of institutional practices, for the effectiveness of education and research, is also problematic. Academic freedom to research and teach without political or 'managerial' interference is a traditional tenet of the academy but does this mean that anything at all can go? Are unengaged teaching and low-quality research, even if rare, acceptable? Surely scholars cannot legitimately see themselves as actors who should be entirely free to follow their own choices and habits, regardless of who is paying their salary, regardless of the values, intentions and standards of the wider research and learning community and regardless of their students' needs. As Ernest Boyer argued, 'scholarship … is a communal act' (Boyer 1996, 16).

There is clearly a tension here between the dangers of an overly dra-conian quality management approach to university life and an entirely personalised academic free-for-all, in which no one is accountable. The pros and cons of quality review principles and processes have been prob-lematised at length in recent literature (Bendermacher et al. 2016), and there is now a promising movement away from an emphasis on 'quality management' towards the development of a shared 'quality culture'. The European University Association (EUA) defines a quality culture as:

> an organisational culture that intends to enhance quality perma-nently and is characterized by two distinct elements: on the one hand, a cultural/psychological element of shared values, beliefs, expectations and commitment towards quality and on the other hand, a structural/managerial element with defined processes that enhance quality and aim at coordinating individual efforts. (EUA 2006, 10)

Finding any kind of structure or coordination that can rest upon shared values may be particularly difficult in university environments, not least because they are made up of academic 'microclimates' (Roxå and Mårtensson 2011). Leading the way at institutional level is a complex process. It needs to build on social identity, as Haslam, Reicher and Platow (2011) argue:

> the leader has no privileged position in providing answers, but serves instead to make collective conversations possible. (Haslam, Reicher and Platow 2011, 217)

The Connected Curriculum approach rests on a commitment to such collective conversations at a time of 'supercomplexity' (Barnett 2000) and of change in higher education and society. It builds on the premise that research and student education are, or need to be, closely related, that researchers, educators, students and practitioners can all benefit from mutual engagement and dialogue, and that institutions need to provide times and spaces for these discussions to take place. This is, of course, not a new position. It draws on some traditional thinking about research, knowledge and what it means to become educated, which will be reviewed briefly here.

5 Revisiting core principles: the unity of research and teaching

Numerous scholars over the centuries, from von Humboldt and Newman in the nineteenth century to Collini (2012), Brew (2006; 2012), Barnett (2011; 2016) and Marginson (2016) in the twenty-first, have explored the purposes of higher education. Are universities predominantly organisations set up to conduct research which also, along the way, teach students? Is their core mission student education, perhaps with research conducted alongside? Or is there a way of bringing those two endeavours much closer together, finding a new 'ecology' for higher education (Barnett 2011), and new areas of synergy and connection with the world?

Revisiting briefly the history of the modern university could help us address these questions. In the nineteenth century, in the early days of the modern European university, Wilhelm von Humboldt wrote of the necessary connection between education and research. In contrast with Newman's later claim that discovery and teaching are distinct functions

...nd not typically combined (Newman 1852, cited in Marginson 2008), Humboldt saw the university as expressing the unity of research and teaching, highlighting the profound synergies between those activities. In a university, 'the teacher does not exist for the sake of the student; both teacher and student have their common justification in the common pursuit of knowledge' (Humboldt 1809, cited in Morgan 2011).

Humboldt's argument is, at its core, a simple one. Human knowledge is infinite: it is always possible to push the boundaries of what we know. And individuals *should* push these boundaries, holding government to account as they do so. Both research and teaching, or education, should be orientated towards these acts of perpetual discovery.

Education in Humboldt's German tradition is defined with reference to the term *Bildung*, which connotes self-formation or development. The word does not translate easily into English; it has broad connotations of transformation, of developing a valued picture (*Bild*) of oneself and taking steps to achieve that vision. Schneider defines *Bildung* as 'action to create a self that is valuable' (Schneider 2012, 305). Used somewhat differently in different contexts, the term has been adopted positively by some critical theorists, who appreciate its potential for establishing social equalities, but also critiqued by others for its association with liberal education rather than political revolution (Horlacher 2015, 68). At its core, however, the term characterises something fundamental about the nature of human knowledge. Fairfield defines this as the principle of the human mind's remaining 'unsatisfied with what it imagines it knows' (Fairfield 2012, 3). The key here is a disposition to question, to test, to remain open to being wrong and to the power of new evidence and new perspectives.

As the German philosopher Gadamer (2004) argued, at the core of this disposition for remaining open to new understandings is the practice of dialogue. A leading scholar in the field of philosophical hermeneutics, Gadamer wrote at length about 'truth and method', addressing fundamental questions about what it makes sense to say that we know. His work shines a light on both education and research, and on the relationship between them.

Gadamer recognised that we all come into any situation – for example, as a teacher, researcher or student – with prior learning and ready-made assumptions. Our beliefs, values, expectations and responses are affected by our prior experiences, by the cultural and historical contexts we inhabit. As we interpret the signs that we see around us – whether these are found in written texts, in the laboratory or in the actions we observe in the workplace – these prior assumptions come into play.

Interpretation is always necessary in learning, in research and in life, evidence is literally meaningless until someone has ascribed a meaning to it. And it is only through dialogic encounters that our interpretations can be tested and developed further.

Each of us has our own horizon, in any given moment, as we look out on what we know. However, through encounters with others we can start to share what we see and our horizons can begin to broaden, even to merge (*Horizontverschmelzung*). No pure objectivity can be obtained as we are all subjects but, as we hold ourselves open to new possibilities, we advance knowledge through intersubjectivity. This philosophical position does not rest on a single research paradigm, method or learning theory, but on a disposition, a way of being, which precedes and can underpin a wide range of methods of enquiry into the world.

Why is this of particular importance to higher education in the twenty-first century? In what has recently been described as a 'post-truth' era, following a comment by UK politician Michael Gove that 'people in this country have had enough of experts' (*The Telegraph*, 20 June 2016), the practice of remaining open to being wrong and recalibrating one's understandings in the light of new evidence, or of new interpretations of existing evidence, needs to be reasserted. Dialogic encounters are vital; they test our assumptions and extend our knowledge.

This can be seen when research findings are peer reviewed, and when research papers cite the work of others to support or refute their own findings. It is also evident when teachers give feedback to students on their work or as part of in-class or online conversation and when students engage with one another, in person or virtually, in peer study groups. Even in the hard sciences, where the focus of investigation into the natural world rests on a broadly reliable 'scientific method' for discovery, peer review and interpretation form an important role in knowledge-building and in translating new knowledge into changes in practice. Findings and assumptions are revisited, questioned, tested and sometimes revised over time. It is human dialogue that builds not only our capacity to express the landscape of our knowledge but also to create that landscape. Gadamer's term *Verständingung*, or 'coming to an understanding with someone', highlights the collective nature of any area of knowledge.

By contrast, much published literature on teaching in higher education emphasises individual learning. We see this, for example, in studies of individual 'approaches to learning' and 'deep and surface' learning (Marton, Hounsell and Entwistle 1997). Revisiting the notion of *Bildung* begins to shift the emphasis from learning as being an entirely individualised activity to education as a collective endeavour. Biesta argues that learning itself can be characterised as 'responding' (2006, 68), in the sense of responding to a question:

> we can say that someone has learned something *not* when she is able to copy and reproduce what already existed, but when she responds to what is unfamiliar, what is different, what challenges, irritates, or even disturbs. Here learning becomes a creation or an invention, a process of bringing something new into the world: one's own, unique response. (2006, 68)

To become educated involves one's own unique response, then, but in the context of human interaction and relationship. For universities, this redirects our attention to structures and practices that promote and create spaces for shared dialogue, peer review and collaborative learning.

Education is not primarily about individual gain and personal benefit, but about developing a sense of collective engagement and responsibility. Education is not a set of technicalities; it embodies an intellectual and ethical position.

'Good education', in this sense, is about helping to create societies in which citizens value the humanity and rights of others. For Reindal (2013), *Bildung* is about the need 'to take responsibility for the humanity in one's own person' in making a contribution to a collective conversation (Reindal 2013, 537). Reindal cites a letter written by a Holocaust survivor who calls upon teachers not just to promote knowledge but to develop our collective humanity:

> Dear Teacher:
> I am a survivor of a concentration camp. My eyes saw what no man should witness:
> Gas chambers built by learned engineers.
> Children poisoned by educated physicians.
> Infants killed by trained nurses.
> Women and babies shot and burned by high school and college graduates.
> So, I am suspicious of education.
> My request is: Help your students become human.
>
> (From Strom and Parsons 1994, 519–520, cited in Reindal 2013, 538)

This moving extract reminds us that knowledge, and how knowledge is used, is an ethical issue. Irina Bokova, Director-General of UNESCO, writes that:

> There is no more powerful transformative force than education – to promote human rights and dignity, to eradicate poverty and deepen sustainability, to build a better future for all, founded on equal rights and social justice, respect for cultural diversity, and international solidarity and shared responsibility, all of which are fundamental aspects of our common humanity. (UNESCO 2015, 4)

Critical scholars question whether such transformation is possible in a society in which inequalities of opportunity are systemically embedded. Certainly participants in dialogic encounters are affected by where they sit around the metaphorical debating table; the many inequalities embedded in the social structures and practices are lived in our universities, and some voices have more importance ascribed to them than others. Marginalised groups and individuals mix with those who come from backgrounds where it is the norm to see speaking out as an entitlement. There are additional power dynamics at play between teacher and student, and between senior academics, early career academics and professional staff. All of these relations – and the structures and policies that restrict and empower them – need to be revisited if we are to maximise the possibility of meaningful dialogue in which everyone's voice is heard.

The content of our curricula also needs to be interrogated to see whether the knowledge base on which we draw is fully representative of global 'knowledges', including those that have traditionally been marginalised. Drawing on the notion of education as *Bildung,* with its goal of transforming individuals *and* societies and its relevance to both education and research, can direct our attention to the task of creating better spaces for people to develop authentic human connections. This includes developing opportunities for participants – students, teachers, researchers, professionals – to address explicitly issues of inequality and inclusion in their thinking and practices. There is a growing awareness that social categorisations such as race, class and gender intersect to create overlapping and interdependent systems of discrimination or disadvantage: universities need to recognise this 'intersectionality' and its impact upon their work.

'Good' education has too often been defined entirely in terms of whether individual students are meeting pre-determined learning outcomes. Framed with reference to values, it can instead be defined as the development of new understandings and practices, through dialogue and human relationships, which make an impact for good in the world.

This framing of education as being *for* society connects it very closely with research. Higher education institutions achieve extraordinary advancements of knowledge through research, both within and across disciplines. Many of these address complex global challenges, including those relating to health and wellbeing and to environmental and cultural sustainability. Right across the disciplines – in natural sciences, technologies, medicine, the social sciences, the arts and the humanities – research produces knowledge that 'enhances our culture and civilisation and can be used for the public good' (Nurse 2015, 2). Connecting education and research is not only to recognise their common ground of advancing knowledge through dialogic encounters, but also to recognise their common goal: to contribute to 'the global common good' (UNESCO 2015). This values-based, theoretical position underpins the Connected Curriculum initiative.

6 Higher education curriculum revisited

In recent years, many institutions around the world have been addressing the design and content of their curricula (Barnett and Coate 2005; Blackmore and Kandiko 2012). Efforts have been made to characterise key components and outcomes – for example, in the UK via the Quality Assurance Agency (QAA) Subject Benchmarks (QAA 2016a), through the European Bologna process (European Commission/EACEA/Eurydice 2015) which has set out to harmonise levels of study across national borders, and through the international AHELO project with its focus on developing shared definitions of 'learning outcomes' (Tremblay, Lalancette and Roseveare 2012). Such initiatives can create opportunities for useful dialogue about curriculum across institutional and national borders, but it is not easy to fit curriculum into neat boxes, even where that is thought to be desirable.

The task of conceptualising curriculum, of pinning it down in some way, has become all the more complex in the modern era of 'blended learning', when much of what is learned can occur online, both within and beyond the parameters of the planned curriculum. The curriculum as it is *lived* by students, in an information age of open access resources and social media, almost inevitably stretches beyond the specifics of what is planned and 'delivered' by programme teams.

When the word 'curriculum' is used in the context of higher education, it is still often seen as a set of components to be addressed, however. This definition is a typical example:

> The term *curriculum,* broadly defined, includes goals for student learning (skills, knowledge and attitudes); content (the subject matter in which learning experiences are embedded); sequence (the order in which concepts are presented); learners; instructional methods and activities; instructional resources (materials and settings); evaluation (methods used to assess student learning as a result of these experiences); and adjustments to teaching and learning processes, based on experience and evaluation. (Dezure et al. 2002)

Issues of curriculum design and structure are important and will be revisited (Chapter 4), but what happens if we define curriculum instead as 'the interplay of all those involved' (Barnett and Coate 2005, 159). What happens if we do *not* frame curriculum design primarily as a technical task but as a cultural imperative to foster productive human dialogue? The implications for educators and researchers in universities today would be significant. The commonly accepted concept of Biggs's 'constructive alignment' (Biggs 2003), whereby every feature of provision must be explicitly aligned to the predetermined learning outcomes, has its own internal logic but it has its limitations. We need also to consider whether curriculum design is enhancing the dynamic exchange of meanings between diverse members of our learning and research communities:

> Management structures and policies, education strategies, curriculum design, patterns of delivery and new initiatives such as learning technologies can thus all be evaluated in terms of their impact on productive, creative relations and communications across the university community. (Fung 2007, 223)

There are, here, implications for *how* we teach. If we conceive of what we are doing as handing out knowledge to students in a one-directional pattern of delivery, we are missing the fundamental principle of education as relational and dialogic. As von Humboldt noted, education should not be about 'piling up unconnected facts', and educators who take this approach are 'betraying [the] cause of learning' (cited in Morgan 2011, 331). It is critical human dialogue which tests and extends our knowledge.

This means that, in the context of internationalised higher education and a values-based commitment to global engagement, we need to:

- Continuously expose students and staff to multiple views of the world (create different socio-cultural/educational societies, promote interdisciplinary activities, harness experiences of all the students in teaching and learning, value alternative world views, use comparative approaches to teaching).
- Seek to create a culture that makes students and staff feel that the university is a democratic meeting place where the encounter of diversity (in terms of gender, maturity, culture, nationality) creates opportunities to develop new competencies, knowledge and understandings.
- Increase opportunities for collaborative learning (communities of practice, group work, workshops, seminars) which exploit the diversity within the student body. (Welikala 2011)

Higher education institutions need to focus on building connected learning and research communities in which every individual can find spaces not only to extend their knowledge horizons and perspectives but also to have a voice. As William Pinar (2012) argues, the emphasis of curriculum should not be on narrowly formulated objectives and standardised testing but on empowering both students and teachers to develop and express their own identities, whereby 'scholarship can enable them to speak' (Pinar 2012, 22).

The underpinning principles of extending understandings through investigative, dialogic encounters and directing new knowledge to the common good may be shared by many but what does this mean in practice for the ways in which curriculum is designed? We turn next to the core principle of the Connected Curriculum framework, that of empowering students to learn through research and active enquiry, and look at how this can strengthen practice.

2
Learning through research and enquiry

1 Research-based education in diverse disciplines

The Connected Curriculum framework is built around a core prop osition: that curriculum should be 'research-based'. That is, the predominant mode of student learning on contemporary degre programmes should reflect the kinds of active, critical and ana lytic enquiry undertaken by researchers. Where possible, student should engage in activities associated with research and thereb develop their abilities to think like researchers, both in groups an independently. These activities may include not only undertakin investigations and formulating related critical arguments and find ings, but also peer review, dissemination of knowledge and publi engagement. Such approaches can apply at all levels of study, fror the first undergraduate year.

Where possible, embedding research and enquiry into programm design includes enabling students to generate new knowledge throug data gathering and analysis, to disseminate their findings to others, an to refine their new understandings through feedback on that dissem nation. The extent to which generating new knowledge is possible wi depend upon disciplinary context but it is more feasible than ever befor at a time when it is possible for so many to reach into a pocket and pu out a mobile device which connects to 4.66 billion Web pages and risin (Pappas 2016). 'Citizen science', part of the Open Science movemen can involve the public in gathering data in remote regions of the plane or crowdsourcing ideas over the internet (LERU 2016). The rapid deve opment of Open Educational Resources is also widening access to higl quality resources, so that many people are 'able to learn about topic which interest them and which are relevant to their lives, irrespectiv of their geographical location, financial status, educational background, and/or other life commitments' (Coughlan and Perryman 2011, 11). Students in one institution now have access to countless resources produced by other institutions, as well as those created by other individuals and organisations.

Of course, social and economic inequalities mean that not all students globally have access to the digital world; this is an important issue that the higher education sector must address. And 'information' in the public sphere can certainly be misinformation, in a challenging era of so-called 'alternative facts' and 'fake news'. But addressing these issues directly with students is a key part of developing their understanding of how knowledge is not always democratically available, of how it is formed and communicated, and of how it must be tested and critically interrogated.

In practice, the design of research-based education is likely to vary considerably across disciplines. This is not only because of the ways in which disciplines have developed distinctive learning and teaching cultures over time but because *research* is defined and practised differently across disciplines (Elken and Wollscheid 2016). Angela Brew found that there has been relatively little scholarly work on investigating conceptions of research (Brew 2001), and discussions of what good research is and how it links with student education have been limited. She argues that:

> There is no one thing, nor a set of things which research is … It cannot be reduced to any kind of essential quality. (Brew 2001, 21)

In her own research, Brew found that experienced researchers tend to conceive of research using 'Domino', 'Trading', 'Layering' and 'Journeying' metaphors.

- The Domino conception suggests that some see research as a series of separate tasks to be completed in sequence.
- Trading refers to the strong focus some have on research in terms of its products – for example, publications – which are then traded for kudos and promotion.
- The Layering conception suggests that research is about uncovering or unearthing that which is hidden.
- The Journeying focus sees research as personally developmental: research informs our individual and collective journeys.

Meyer, Shanahan and Laughksch (2005), drawing on Brew in a later study, find that students typically conceive academic research to be one or more of the following:

- the gathering of information or collection of data;
- the discovery of truth;
- an insightful process of exploration and discovery, leading to a deeper understanding of the topic;
- the uncovering of what has been hidden, through reinterpretation or 're-search'.

Åkerlind (2008) notes that variations in conceptions of research can be characterised by differences in:

- research intentions (who is affected by the research);
- research outcomes (the anticipated impact of the research);
- research questions (the nature of the object of study);
- research process (how research is undertaken); and
- researcher affect (underlying feelings about research).

(Åkerlind 2008, 13)

Åkerlind's analysis of the experiences and perceptions of academics led to her strongly questioning the assumption that 'academics of similar prestige and seniority in similar disciplines must hold a similar view of the nature of research and quality in research', and she noted that such variations are 'typically hidden' (Åkerlind 2008, 30).

Disciplinary differences do, however, play a part in how research is conceived and practised. Much has been written over the years about disciplinary variations, and these come into play directly when we consider how curriculum can be based on the principles and practices of research. Becher drew on an anthropological study of academia to write his influential work on academic 'tribes and territories' (Becher 1989). By the time Becher and Trowler published a second edition of this text (2001), they noted that, in the intervening decades, there had been major shifts in the topography of academic knowledge. However, their typology of four different kinds of discipline as 'hard pure' (e.g. physics), 'soft-pure' (e.g. history; anthropology), 'hard-applied' (e.g. mechanical engineering; clinical medicine) and 'soft-applied' (e.g. business studies; education) remains relevant (Jessop and Maleckar 2016). The typology has prompted further analysis of the ways in which the four broad disciplinary groupings are characterised by different approaches to teaching and student assessment.

Neumann, Parry and Becher (2002, 406–408) found that, in hard-pure disciplines, for example, curriculum is often 'conceived as linear and hierarchical, building up brick by brick towards contemporary knowledge'. In these disciplines, content is 'typically fixed, cumulative and quantitatively measured, with the teaching and learning activities being focused and instructive: the emphasis is typically upon the teacher informing the student'. In sharp contrast, they say, 'content in soft-pure disciplines tends to be more free-ranging and qualitative, with knowledge-building a formative process and teaching and learning activities largely constructive and interpretative'. Knowledge communities working in applied disciplines tend to be 'gregarious, with multiple influences and interactions on both their teaching and research activity'.

Approaches to student assessment vary, too. Neumann, Parry and Becher (2002) find that hard-pure subjects are often orientated towards assessing students through closely-focused examination questions, while soft-pure subjects favour continuous assessments which allow for more nuanced and extended expressions of ideas. In soft-pure and soft-applied fields, essays and project-based assessments are more commonplace, as are self-assessments and peer-assessments; these 'emphasise knowledge application and integration, usually in essay or explanatory form' (Neumann, Parry and Becher 2002, 408).

It is unsurprising that different customs and practices have arisen in different fields, as disciplinary groupings are characterised by different ideas of knowledge, or epistemologies. Those who apply scientific method, seeing knowledge as in principle generalisable and replicable, have a different orientation towards knowledge – and therefore research – than those who see it as relative, culturally specific, mediated by the slipperiness of language and value-laden. Those whose focus is on the natural world can study its objects but those who research human experience study subjects, who have their own agency and voice.

Becher and Trowler (2001) observe that the changing demands on higher education, emergent affinities between traditional subjects to address complex conceptual, social and economic issues and the development of new degree subjects – for example, in relation to the digital domain – mean that these broad distinctions have become blurred in many contexts. However, customary differences need to be recognised in any consideration of curriculum development that aims to base student education on research.

How then does the link between research-based education and research differ in different kinds of discipline? Each discipline needs to consider its own orientation. For example, the relationship between research and education in professional disciplines such as medicine and engineering has particular characteristics. Here, research typically has a focus on improving professional practice, and student education is directed at producing effective, confident, evidence-informed professionals. Enabling students to learn through research and enquiry equips them specifically with the skills and approaches they will need to operate effectively in a specified professional role. The notion of research-based education is thus relatively straightforward. This may also be so in other practice-related fields, including the creative arts, where practice itself can be seen as a form of enquiry, of pushing the edges of what it is possible to know, think, feel and do.

The relationship can play out rather differently however in 'pure' humanities subjects. A study by Ochsner, Hug and Daniel (2012) highlights four types of research in the humanities:

- positively connoted 'traditional' research (characterised as individual, discipline-oriented, and ground-breaking research);
- positively connoted 'modern' research (characterised as cooperative, interdisciplinary, and having societal relevance);
- negatively connoted 'traditional' research (characterised as isolated, reproductive, and conservative);
- negatively connoted 'modern' research (characterised as career-oriented, epigonal, calculated). (Ochsner, Hug and Daniel. 2012, 2)

Collaborative studies are becoming more common in some humanities fields but the predominantly individual, rather than team-based, nature of humanities research distinguishes it from the natural sciences. A question to consider for humanities departments is whether students can, during their degree, learn through emulating the research activities undertaken by a range of different kinds of researchers in the field, and, where possible, by 'visiting' researchers and questioning them on their work (see Chapter 3). Preparing students to investigate in groups as well as individually, to experience peer review and to present new findings and arguments to diverse audiences can all be very beneficial for their learning.

In fields such as Literary Studies and Philosophy, where the objects of focus for both research and study are typically texts, critically analysing text is fundamental to both research and to learning: in this sense research and learning are already closely aligned, even conflated. Research-based education in this context may mean, however, putting an even greater emphasis on designing sequences of research questions, on problematising analyses and arguments, and on developing and using different kinds of theoretical framing.

With the advent of new technologies, researchers who engage with texts increasingly undertake innovative activities to extend the edge of knowledge, for example by making use of new analytical software or even through focusing on digital humanities as a field of study. They may in turn develop new theoretical framings through which established as well as new texts can be examined. Departments may want to consider whether students are finding out about, and where possible participating in, the full range of emerging, research-related activities in their field.

Thus, research practices have a spectrum of characteristics across disciplines. These include, for example, critical analysis of primary and secondary texts; critiquing and practising creative arts; laboratory-based experiments; investigations into and/or involving the public; analysis of physical and/or social phenomena via field trips; object-based investigations; complex, interdisciplinary, problem-solving challenges; and evidence-informed analysis of professional practice. The Connected Curriculum framework's emphasis on developing new opportunities for learning through building active questioning and critical dialogue into the fabric of the curriculum design, from the first day of the programme of study to the last, relates to and can strengthen any and all research practices. It is within the gift of institutions, departments and programme teams to consider what 'research and enquiry' are and can be in the given context, and to empower students to consider this question for themselves.

The shared underpinning principle is that all disciplines need to investigate the opportunities we have in a technology-rich world to move away from some of the traditional teaching methods that situated students, deliberately or inadvertently, as passive recipients of a canon of fixed knowledge towards a more enquiry-based model. This entails designing learning activities that empower students to think and act like researchers. Where practices of research differ across disciplines, then the ways in which students study and learn will vary between disciplines, perhaps even more than they do at present.

A range of specific ways in which students can learn through connecting with research and researchers is characterised in Chapter 3 (Table 3.1). However, as Jenkins notes, we will always need to continue to 'develop our understanding of the diverse and heterogeneous ways in which teaching and research are linked' (Jenkins 2004, 5).

The Connected Curriculum approach puts questions about definitions of research back into the court of academics, within their discipline and across interdisciplinary groupings: for *you*, what is research? What would engaging students in research and enquiry, and thereby strengthening both their learning and your group's research, look like in *your* context?

But on what basis is the claim made that research and active enquiry *should* be even more central to students' learning opportunities? What evidence is there that connecting students with research and enabling them to participate in its practices, even as undergraduates, is beneficial to their learning and to the ways in which they experience their time at university? Defining and examining 'teaching excellence' and 'what works' is conceptually and empirically complex, but examining research-informed literature is important. We begin with the wider conceptual arguments made by scholars relating to the relationship between research, scholarship and education, and then look more closely at empirical evidence for the effectiveness of research-based practices in different disciplines.

2 Scholarly perspectives from academic literature

Conceptual and theoretical framings

A number of scholarly publications have influenced conceptual reframings of the relationships between research and student education. In the United States, the argument for bringing students closer to research has been influenced by the Boyer Commission (1998), which furthers earlier work on academic scholarship and engagement by Ernest Boyer (1990; 1996). Boyer proposed a broad conception of scholarship for university academics which recognises that original research (discovery) needs to be linked closely with a scholarly approach to the integration and application of ideas, and to teaching itself:

Surely, scholarship means engaging in original research. But the work of the scholar also means stepping back from one's investigation, looking for connections, building bridges between theory and practice, and communicating one's knowledge effectively to students. (Boyer 1990, 16)

The Boyer Commission subsequently published a paper emphasising the importance of engaging all students in research; students brought into a scholarly community need to participate fully in its culture. The focus in the paper is on research-intensive institutions, and the authors argue that these universities need to create a 'synergistic system' from which both students and research will benefit:

Undergraduates who enter research universities should understand the unique quality of the institutions and the concomitant opportunities to enter a world of discovery in which they are active participants, not passive receivers. ... Collaborative learning experiences provide alternative means to share in the learning experiences, as do the multitudinous resources available through the computer. The skills of analysis, evaluation, and synthesis will become the hallmarks of a good education, just as absorption of a body of knowledge once was. (Boyer Commission 1998, 20)

This paper offers 'An Academic Bill of Rights', which proposes that students in any kind of college or university should have opportunities to learn through enquiry, to develop excellent communication skills, to appreciate arts, humanities and social sciences, and to be well prepared for future life and employment. The authors propose that students in a research university, however, have these additional rights:

- expectation of and opportunity for work with talented senior researchers to help and guide the student's effort;
- access to first-class facilities in which to pursue research – laboratories, libraries, studios, computer systems, and concert halls;
- many options among fields of study and directions to move within those fields, including areas and choices not found in other kinds of institutions;
- opportunities to interact with people of backgrounds, cultures, and experiences which differ from the student's own, and with

pursuers of knowledge at every level of accomplishment, from freshmen students to senior research faculty. (Boyer Commission 1998, 22)

The Boyer Commission (2001) subsequently published the results of a survey of ninety-one US research institutions. Developments in curricula had been reported and all of these universities offered some opportunities for students to engage in supervised research or creative activities. However, the extent to which students were in fact engaged with these was very variable, with many saying that this was true of few of their undergraduates.

A comparable set of principles is presented in a position paper developed on behalf of the League of European Research Universities (LERU) (Fung, Besters-Dilger and van der Vaart 2017). This paper draws on a survey of twenty-three research-intensive institutions from across Europe to examine the notion of excellent education in research-rich universities. It argues that 'excellence', in this context, is characterised by regular and meaningful opportunities to engage with research and researchers, within and across disciplines, and to develop a wide range of related ethical values and skills that can be transferred to diverse contexts:

[B]eing part of a research-rich culture benefits students by providing them with a range of approaches to knowledge and knowledge production. These relate to the learning that occurs when undertaking the specific academic, cultural and professional practices of particular disciplines and/or of thematic interdisciplinary investigations. Benefits for students also arise from the intellectual depth associated with engaging in any cutting edge investigations, and from the range of skills associated with independent and collaborative enquiry. (Fung, Besters-Dilger and van der Vaart 2017, 5)

However, it is not only in research-focused institutions that many of the underpinning principles of research-based education come into play. While research-intensive universities, with their greater research volume, can typically offer more access to researchers whose work is taking place at the leading edge of global knowledge in a field, institutions that do not have a primary focus on research can also comprise scholarly learning communities that engage students in active, critical enquiry. The US Council on Undergraduate Research is a body committed to the principle of learning through research and promotes developments in undergraduate research opportunities across all types of institution. Its online publication, The Council on Undergraduate Research Quarterly (CURQ 2016), has published numerous 'real world' studies, including international case studies, in which varieties of undergraduate research are presented and analysed. These give scholarly and also practical insights into the challenges and benefits of constructing curricula in such a way that they enable students to participate in research.

However, Brew (2006) shows just how divided, conceptually and in practice, research and student education have been in many institutions (Figure 2.1). She argues that traditionally academic researchers have been orientated very much towards knowledge generation, while teaching has been characterised by knowledge transmission.

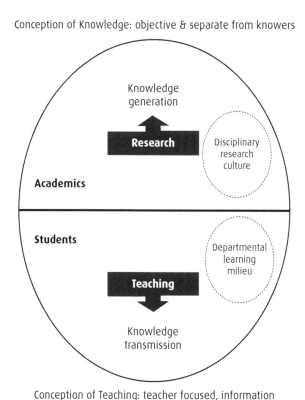

Fig. 2.1 Traditional model of the relationship between teaching and research (Brew 2006, 18)

Brew argues this old division is inappropriate; there are many nuanced connections between research and teaching, and between academics and their students, that need to be cultivated (Fig.2.2).

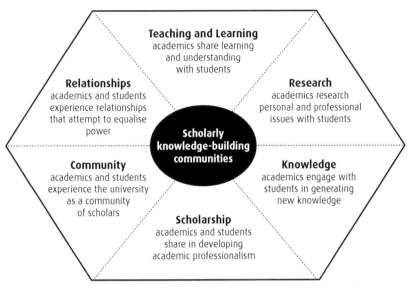

Fig. 2.2   New model of the relationship between teaching and research. (Adapted from Brew 2006, 32)

Analysing the various strands of scholarly activity and their synergies, Brew makes the case that we need to 'define a new kind of higher education in which students, academics and others who work in universities progressively work towards the development of inclusive scholarly knowledge-building communities of practice' (Brew 2006, 180).

Healey and Jenkins (2009, 3) also propose that research opportunities within the undergraduate curriculum 'should and can be mainstreamed for all or many students', regardless of the type of institution. They have conceptualised four main ways of engaging undergraduates with research and enquiry:

- **research-led**: learning about current research in the discipline;
- **research-oriented**: developing research skills and techniques;
- **research-based**: undertaking research and inquiry;
- **research-tutored**: engaging in research discussions.

(Healey and Jenkins 2009, 6)

Healey and Jenkins focus in particular on promoting 'research-based' and 'research-oriented' approaches to teaching, in which students undertake research and enquiry and develop associated skills and techniques. They note that 'research-led' models, in which students hear about research, and 'research-tutored' approaches, in which they engage in research-focused discussions, are also valuable but emphasise the benefits of approaches which position students as active learners.

Levy and Petrulis (2012, 86) take a fresh look at the conceptual assumptions behind enquiry-based learning. They argue for moving beyond 'active learning' models, useful as they are, to a more comprehensive conceptualisation which includes 'real' research. Drawing on Barnett's work, they emphasise the value to students of engaging in research: the development of critical and reflexive qualities needed 'in a profoundly uncertain, supercomplex world'. They also draw on Brew to emphasise the value of students being able to work in partnership with staff, an approach which 'fosters dispositions and intellectual and practical capabilities of particular importance to life and work in contemporary society'.

Developing a new conceptual framework, Levy and Petrulis identify four types of enquiry-based learning: *identifying, pursuing, producing and authoring*. The first two are associated with exploring existing knowledge, while the latter two move into the realm of building new knowledge.

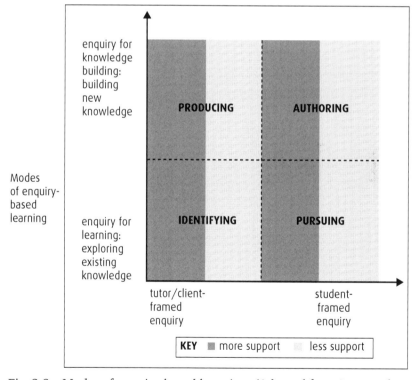

Fig. 2.3   Modes of enquiry-based learning. (Adapted from Levy and Petrulis 2012, 97)

The core principle of the Connected Curriculum framework, 'Students learn through research and enquiry', speaks to all four of these dimensions but with a particular emphasis on taking steps towards the 'authoring' dimension, to maximise student ownership and voice.

Levy and Petrulis make valuable references to socio-economic and cultural factors on student education here. They point to a range of studies taking wider theoretical perspectives, including work on 'students as producers' by Neary and Winn (2009), who draw on critical theory and whose goal is to democratise knowledge production. They also highlight work by Baxter-Magolda (2004) on the importance of students having 'self-authorship', which includes 'belief in oneself as possessing the capacity to create new knowledge' and 'the ability to play a part within knowledge-building communities' (Levy and Petrulis 2012, 87).

There are echoes here of education framed as *Bildung* which, as we saw earlier, emphasises individual and collective 'becoming'. But there are also important reminders of the critical hermeneutic tradition in which critical theorists such as Jürgen Habermas highlight the damaging inequalities that result from contemporary political and economic systems:

> Some members of society, because of their class position, racial identity, and education, have greater access to information and hence greater life chances than others. (Habermas 1996, 5)

In arguing for the central importance of learning through research and enquiry, critical questions about definitions of 'good' or 'excellent' education come to the fore once again: is 'excellent education' about efficiently and effectively acquiring a pre-set body of knowledge and skills? Is it about producing people who can generate economic success for their society? The emphasis in the Connected Curriculum framing is on developing oneself according to one's vision and values, and on self-authorship for the purpose of developing a good society. The focus here is not limited to achieving planned learning outcomes and economic success, as useful as these may be; it foregrounds the importance of developing critical citizens, who challenge social structures and what is currently 'known'.

These are vital issues for society and for participants in higher education today: their very complexity and importance point us back to the need not only for engaging students in critical enquiry but also for creating spaces for faculty members to debate these themes, within and across disciplines. The Connected Curriculum framework can become a catalyst for such dialogue even in a large, multi-disciplinary institution (Chapter 9).

3 Empirical evidence for 'effectiveness'

Although there are many theoretical and conceptual lenses through which to view the principle of 'learning through research and enquiry', it is useful to evaluate existing empirical evidence of the effectiveness of research-based curriculum design in given contexts. 'Effectiveness' is a signifier that shifts according to context and values, of course, but it is an important one to address.

To illustrate the growing body of literature on the impact of research-based curriculum design, we examine first science-orientated studies by Nobel Laureate Carl Wieman (2016a) and his colleagues. We then consider more qualitative studies focusing on arts, humanities and social science disciplines (Blessinger and Carfora eds. 2014; Wood 2010; Spronken-Smith and Walker 2010; Levy and Petrulis 2012).

In the sciences, the number of examples of empirical research into improvements to students' learning is growing. A series of empirical studies has been undertaken in the United States in recent years in connection with the work of Carl Wieman (2016a), Professor of Physics at Stanford University, in disciplines including chemistry, computer science, geography, life sciences, mathematics, physics, astronomy and statistics: see, for example, Arthurs and Templeton 2009, Smith et al. 2011, Dohaney, Brogt and Kennedy 2012, Hoskinson, Caballero and Knight 2013.

Wieman and Gilbert (2015, 152–156) synthesise a number of the findings by researchers into active, enquiry-based learning in the natural and applied sciences. Citing studies in cognitive psychology, they note three common components to the scientific disciplines:

- a large amount of specialised knowledge;
- a specific mental organisational framework, unique to the field of expertise;
- monitoring one's own thinking and learning in the field of expertise.

They emphasise the importance of being able to apply knowledge to problem solving and the need for 'deliberate practice', defined as 'a common process required for developing expertise'. Enabling students to apply knowledge actively and to engage in deliberate practice requires the setting up of active tasks, not simply the passive reception of knowledge or repetition of established processes. Wieman and Gilbert argue that the specific areas of expertise to be developed in any area of science include:

- recognising and using concepts and mental models and developing sophisticated selection criteria for deciding when specific models are applicable;
- recognising relevant and irrelevant information for solving a problem;
- knowing and applying a set of criteria for evaluating whether or not a result or conclusion makes sense;
- moving fluently among specialised representations such as graphs, equations, and specialised diagrams.

Their argument is that teachers in science disciplines need to maximise the amount of deliberate practice by students in these areas: to 'design suitable tasks that provide authentic practice of expert skills for the students at the appropriate level of challenge'. Feedback on students' practice, peer learning and discussions among faculty members about the best approaches are all seen to be critically important in order to improve student performance.

Wieman and Gilbert cite a number of studies which use quantitative measures and inventories to demonstrate that significant learning gain is achieved through devising methods of active enquiry and feedback, including using systems of peer instruction based on questioning during classes and small group work. They note that, when this method was introduced on four core courses in computer science, there was 'a dramatic decrease in the drop and failure rates across all four courses'.

In a related study, an experiment was set up to teach two large, comparable cohorts at the University of British Columbia using different methods. One group was taught by an experienced professor (with good previous evaluations), and the other was taught more experimentally, by a PhD graduate who had been trained in the principles of research-based learning. Both shared the same planned learning objectives and had the same class time. Wieman and Gilbert detail the experiment: in brief, the students who had to engage in interactive, research-based methods and received feedback from fellow students and their instructor were later tested in a quiz designed to 'probe the mastery of the learning objectives'. They outperformed the other, traditionally taught, student cohort significantly: 'The difference in performance between the control and experimental section is very large – an effect of 2.5 standard deviations – and is reflected in the entire distribution'. The authors cite a number of similar studies, emphasising the benefit to students' learning and the improvement in measured levels of active engagement with the course.

Collectively these science-orientated studies make the case in favour of active enquiry. But it is not only in the sciences that scholars are investigating the impact of research- and enquiry-based interventions. Blessinger and Carfora (eds. 2014) present case studies that illustrate the value of enquiry-based learning across arts, humanities and social sciences programmes. The case studies, drawn from a number of national settings, demonstrate a range of enquiry-based approaches but Blessinger and Carfora find that 'the ongoing interaction and relationship between instructor and learner, as well as between learners' (2014, 5) is consistently important. This finding reflects the hermeneutic principle that dialogue is the key to developing understandings (Chapter 1). It is human interaction that allows the questioning and testing of prior knowledge and the development of new knowledge: that is, the widening and even merging of knowledge horizons.

'Learning through research and enquiry' is not about sending individual students off into the unknown to fend for themselves intellectually but setting up structured opportunities for investigation that are infused with human interactions, peer learning and peer review. These interactions can increasingly empower diverse students to speak out as engaged members of their learning and research community.

Blessinger and Carfora (2014, 6–7) infer from the case studies they present that there needs to be 'a shift in mindset and attitude' with regard to the roles of teacher and student. They emphasise the importance of encouraging students to 'develop meaningful questions' and 'determine what resources, actions, knowledge and skills are needed to help answer those questions'. Through these processes, students 'learn to use logic, reasoning, and argumentation as well as creativity and judgment'.

Jamie Wood (2010) offers a meta-analytical study focused on enquiry-based learning in the arts and humanities, drawing on impact data from a number of institutionally funded enquiry-based developments in the arts and humanities at the University of Sheffield. He draws on nine projects (from a data set of 56), selected to reflect a spectrum of disciplines and approaches. Undertaking qualitative analysis, he finds a range of important elements in the learning design, including the design of learning spaces and student assessments. Overall, he concludes that students' attitudes towards learning and towards their disciplines improve through engaging in enquiry-based learning. Wood emphasises the need for appropriate levels of support for students during their investigations, particularly when undertaking group work and at the earlier levels of study (Wood 2010, 35).

Spronken-Smith and Walker (2010) draw on three case studies – from medicine, political communications and ecology – to analyse the impact of enquiry-based approaches. They characterise these as approaches in which learning is:

- stimulated by enquiry, i.e. driven by questions or problems;
- based on a process of constructing knowledge and new understanding;
- an 'active' approach, involving learning by doing;
- a student-centred approach to teaching in which the role of the teacher is to act as a facilitator; and
- a move to self-directed learning with students taking increasing responsibility for their learning.

Spronken-Smith and Walker (2010, 723–738) draw on work by Jerome Bruner and Lev Vygotsky to address the importance of 'scaffolding' students' learning, by providing structured support for them to build up their levels of independence as they investigate. They distinguish between three levels of enquiry:

- structured inquiry – where teachers provide an issue or problem and an outline for addressing it;
- guided inquiry – where teachers provide questions to stimulate inquiry but students are self-directed in terms of exploring these questions;
- open inquiry – where students formulate the questions themselves as well as going through the full inquiry cycle.

Using an interpretist paradigm and mixed methods of data collection to gather empirical evidence, they find that:

> if teachers are aiming for strong links between teaching and research, they should adopt an open, discovery-oriented

inquiry-based approach. However, more structured and guided forms of inquiry can be useful to progressively develop particular skills.

They find also that if teachers engage as co-constructors of knowledge, this helps to 'facilitate an academic community of practice including both academics and students'.

We see through these illustrative examples of empirical research that there is a range of evidence – developed through various methodological approaches and focused on different disciplinary applications of enquiry-based learning – to suggest that educational value is seen across a wide range of contexts. There are strong indications that students are more engaged and more able to apply their learning when they undertake enquiry-based activities. Important for the success of research-based education is providing sufficient support through the levels of study – moving from more guidance to more freedom – and building regular peer interaction (including collaboration, peer feedback and peer review) into the learning design.

4 Global perspectives and cultural specificity

The learning contexts addressed so far have varied in discipline. However, they have not varied very widely in terms of the range of global settings and types of educational system in which higher education programmes of study take place. Much of the work in this field has taken place in the UK, Northern Europe, Australasia and the United States. Recent studies have critiqued the geographically narrow focus of the scholarship that addresses teaching and learning in higher education. Edmore Mutekwe (2015), for example, argues that Africa's 'indigenous education systems' have often been ignored, and that:

> the advent of [the] modern type of western education has resulted in the dearth of the importance of indigenous forms of knowledge in Africa. (2015, 1294)

Mutekwe asks whether indigenous knowledge education systems could be 'used to foster an Afrocentric philosophy of Education'. Yusef Waghid (2014, 1), in his book *African Philosophy of Education Reconsidered,* also argues for a distinctive African philosophy of education, one 'guided by communitarian, reasonable and culture-dependent action'.

Hoon and Looker (2013, 131) consider three types of exclusion experienced by Asian participants and their perspectives from the dominant literature on teaching and learning in higher education: 'geographical isolation, methodological solipsism, and ideological exclusion'. They argue that active steps must be taken to 'consciously acknowledge the need for alternative voices that are located outside its immediate realm', and that 'differences in practice, participants, and the politics of culture in locations outside the West need to be taken into consideration'.

The case is well made that the field of scholarship addressing teaching and learning in higher education 'has much to gain by paying attention to and not denying the existence of such enriching, if less familiar, perspectives' and these principles inform the Connected Curriculum approach (see UCL's Liberating the Curriculum project, UCL 2016g). If students are to widen their knowledge horizons through connecting with those whose orientations to knowledge differ considerably, it is vital to open up dialogue about what research and enquiry might, and might not, be in and across different national and cultural settings. People and peoples across the world need to have a voice, including those who have become displaced as a result of global developments and conflicts. In the literature search referred to here, diverse voices are not well represented; however, the international community is fully included in the Connected Curriculum's intention to find a pathway to better dialogue, better global engagement and understandings.

The origins of the Connected Curriculum framework are also rooted in *research-intensive* universities in the UK. Many of the examples of practice provided in the following chapters are from such institutions. In these contexts, cutting-edge research is both prestigious and plentiful. How might the dimensions of the framework play out differently in institutions where this is not the case? This is for those institutions to judge but the core emphasis on students becoming actively engaged with research and enquiry has the potential to apply to many educational contexts.

The underpinning premise, that enhancing students' opportunities to engage with and in authentic research and enquiry is beneficial, is not just a pedagogical orientation: it is a values-based, philosophical orientation highlighting the importance of dialogue, relationship and the ability to continue to question what we think we know, within and across our disciplinary, institutional, cultural and national borders. This principle runs through all six of the associated dimensions of the framework, to which we now turn.

3

Enabling students to connect with researchers and research

Introduction

The first dimension of the Connected Curriculum framework is that of enabling students to connect with research and researchers. The distinctiveness of research universities is that areas of knowledge, analysis and practice, across a wide range of academic disciplines and professional fields, are constantly being enlarged and refreshed. This research is extraordinarily rich and varied, both in terms of its areas of focus and of the activities that researchers undertake. Through research, new understandings, practices and technologies are developed, skills are honed, and ethical issues are uncovered. These can all have a powerful effect not only on researchers themselves but on wider society. Yet students are not always familiar with the research being undertaken in the sector, in their own institution or even in the department in which they are studying. The first dimension thus encourages departments, programme teams and students to look for new ways of building connections between students, researchers and their research.

Revisiting learning design

The extent to which students can connect with research and researchers will be affected by ways in which they experience their programme as a whole: the range of types of class (or online equivalent) they experience, the ways in which their learning is assessed, and the extra-curricular opportunities provided by the department or institution. With the advent of online learning environments, traditional teaching modes such as lecturing, seminars and tutorials are being used more flexibly. This can also open up new possibilities for students to engage with and explore current research. It can be helpful to look first at current practices, then consider how and when students can make the most of studying in a research-rich environment.

It is common in the literature on teaching and learning in higher education to look at teaching methods: how can a lecturer make the best of the 'lecture hour'? How can a seminar tutor get students to engage fully, both in preparation for and during class? How can students work most effectively in a lab, or on a field trip? These are all important questions, and there have been notable developments in approaches in the past decade. These include 'flipped lectures', whereby students watch a video of a lecture, or access key information or ideas through another means, before attending class. The 'lecture' time is then spent undertaking interactive activities, such as collaborating on the development of new arguments or solving problems that relate to the information and ideas accessed beforehand. The use of technologies such as smart phones and interactive audience response 'clickers' can make such activities possible, even with large numbers of students in a traditional lecture theatre.

Other 'blended learning' techniques that mix face-to-face with online activities such as discussion forums and student-created wikis can also involve students very actively in their learning; Evans, Muijs and Tomlinson (2015) summarise a number of useful 'high-impact strategies' for promoting active student engagement in their learning. Many of these enhanced approaches can be used as a flexible platform for introducing students to current research and involving them in its practices and findings, as part of the overall design of the programme.

In some contexts it may be possible to take an even more radical look at whether the traditional lecture and seminar format, or lecture and laboratory format, could be significantly amended. What would happen if students on undergraduate programmes were organised in different ways? What would happen, for example, if they were allocated to research groups on arrival at university and spent a proportion of their first year learning by looking through the lens of that specialism? What would happen if, say, 25 per cent of the learning credits in each year of study were flexibly conceived and allocated directly to learning through and from research, empowering students to have more ownership of their own degree profile and journey? Challenges arise for programmes with large student numbers but even very large cohorts can be divided into small peer groups who can collaborate online or even face-to-face in timetabled sessions (Fung 2007). Access to specialist research spaces and equipment for large numbers of students is likely to be limited, but 'softer' kinds of enquiry, for example into the ways in which research in the field is disseminated and applied, can be undertaken without specialist materials, and institutions are increasingly developing online access to highly specialised research in virtual laboratories (see the fifth vignette of practice which concludes this chapter).

Assessing students' learning is another important issue. What is the pattern of assessments across the whole programme of study? When and how will students receive feedback on their work so that they can learn from that and move forward? Traditional modes of assessment such as essays, portfolios and timed examinations still have their place in the modern university and students benefit from them, but some assessments, including peer assessments and group tasks that mirror the peer review and collaborative projects undertaken by researchers, lend themselves more readily to fostering meaningful connections between students, researchers and research (see Chapter 7). In particular, building collaborative small-group assessments into each year or level of study (Chapter 4) can enable students to work together to investigate research practices and findings.

Some departments or programme teams may be in a position to consider only very minor amendments to their curriculum design, assessment methods and extra-curricular opportunities; others may be willing and able to consider some radical possibilities. In either case, stopping to discuss options for learning design that enable students to connect with research and researchers (Table 3.1) can be fruitful.

3 Practical options for connecting students with research and researchers

The table below (3.1) characterises a range of possibilities for enriching students' opportunities to benefit from being in a research-rich culture, in ways that suit different disciplinary contexts.

There is no 'best' profile of opportunities for students; this will depend very much on the discipline and the context in which they are studying. We will look in more detail at how such activities can be part of a holistically designed programme (Chapter 4), and at how students can produce work which engages different audiences (Chapter 7). The challenge here is to explore, pilot and evaluate activities that can

Table 3.1 Students connect with research and researchers

	Students connect with research and researchers by:	How, where and when?	To what effect?
1 Finding out about research	Exploring what research is, within and/or across disciplines	Before starting their programme of study, online or during a visit day	Improving understanding of the university's mission
	Investigating different research methodologies and associated methods	As part of an induction activity at the start of the programme	Characterising the nature of the discipline(s) and/or professions
	Reading, seeing or hearing about current research studies, both the approaches being undertaken and the emergent findings	As individual preparation for classes	Developing students' overall awareness of how knowledge is created and extended
		During classes, as part of critical analysis in/of the subject	
	Observing research being undertaken in real time (face-to-face or online)	By attending department-wide research seminars	Enabling students to see through different disciplinary 'knowledge lenses'
		Through interdisciplinary projects	
		As part of a 'capstone', synoptic module at the end of the programme	
2 Talking about research	Meeting individual researchers and engaging in dialogue with them	Collaborating with others in a peer study group to study the work of a researcher	Developing students' sense of belonging to an active learning and research community
	Discussing others' research informally through discussion (face-to-face or online)	Undertaking peer review activities in class or online	Increasing motivation and engagement
	Undertaking specific peer review activities	Preparing for formative and summative assessments	Developing confidence in using the language of research
	Participating in events such as seminars and conferences.	Undertaking field trips, visits, explorations of place	Enabling students to contribute questions, insights and critiques from their different personal,
		Contributing to departmental seminar programmes, student research	

3 Doing research	Engaging in collaborative enquiry as part of a peer group Undertaking individual enquiry Undertaking a research project (as part of a team, and individually) Evaluating one's own research, including ethical considerations	Formulating research questions Developing research skills Writing a research 'bid' Carrying out research, including study of relevant literature, analysis of evidence and development of argument Analysing the achievements and limitations of own research, and its place in the field	Building up students' skills and levels of understanding Enabling students to experience the joys and challenges of undertaking a whole project Developing students' skills of evidence-gathering, analysis and evaluation Developing awareness of ethics and values
4 Producing research 'outputs'	Developing awareness of ways in which research is already communicated to others Communicating the findings of own research effectively to different audiences Engaging with different kinds of audience (including alumni), face-to-face or online, to develop ideas in partnership	Considering different audiences for the findings from research Analysing different modes of research communication, including informal modes such as blogs and videos, and formal peer reviewed publications Writing or creating one or more outputs from own research (individually or collaboratively) Analysing and learning from the effectiveness and impact of the outputs Following up with responses from audiences and future opportunities for engagement	Enabling students to develop (transferable) skills needed for 'digital citizenship', including managing own digital identity and ability to work in different media Developing effective oral, written and visual communication skills, including use of different language registers Creation of a body of produced work available to external agencies, such as employers, which gives students a distinctive profile and voice beyond the programme

engage students even more meaningfully with research and researchers. Working in partnership with students or student representatives and interested alumni to discuss the range of appropriate possibilities for the given departmental context (including the discipline and number of students) can be a very productive way forward.

4 Meet the Researcher: a flexible student activity

One activity that can be run either as an extra-curricular project or as part of the formal curriculum is 'Meet the Researcher'. This example builds on work done in the UCL Geography department some years ago, when first-year students were asked to interview a member of the research staff (Dwyer 2001). More recently at UCL, this idea was developed further and promoted across the institution as a student induction activity.

For this activity, students are asked to work in small groups to investigate the work of one of the department's researchers, to meet up with them and to produce some kind of 'output' relating to their findings. The aims, as expressed in a flexible UCL template (UCL 2016b), are to:

- introduce students to the research culture of the department in general and to the work of one researcher in particular;
- help students get to know one another and begin to develop teamwork and project-management skills;
- develop students' abilities to distil, synthesise and communicate key ideas;
- develop their communication skills, including their ability to select appropriate language and media for a specified audience, and enhance related digital practices (for example, the use of presentation slides, video or e-poster).

Students are encouraged to plan carefully for when they meet the researcher and consider the sorts of questions they will ask. These may include, for example:

- What is the researcher trying to achieve, and why?
- What is it like to be a researcher, on a day-to-day basis? What skills are needed?
- What are the highs and lows of research?
- How is the research funded and how is it communicated to the public?

- How will the researcher know when she or he is successful?
- What excites them about their field?

This activity can form the basis of a student induction activity on arrival, which has the advantage of familiarising students with the idea of research in the discipline and also of giving students the opportunity to meet and work meaningfully with a small group of peers from day one, or it can take place later in the programme.

The students' group task, that of creating an artefact of some kind that communicates the work of the researcher to a lay audience, can be treated as a formative, developmental activity or count towards the marks awarded for a given module or unit of study. Giving students the opportunity to select the form of their communications 'artefact' allows groups to share their technical strengths as well as their creativity.

Evaluations of the 'Meet the Researcher' approach have been remarkably positive (see, for example, Standen and Evans 2015), with students appreciating the opportunity to familiarise themselves with some of the department's research, and researchers appreciating the students' interest and the work they have produced when profiling their research.

5 'Only connect': why connecting with research and researchers matters

The value of connecting with research and with researchers can be seen on a number of levels. Students can be very highly motivated by cutting edge thinking in their chosen subjects. Of course, the nature of this will differ widely across disciplines. Students can gain, for example, by observing and working with leading practitioners in the creative arts, or they can benefit from working alongside experimental chemists or physicists in a laboratory. They can have their eyes opened by contributing in some way to clinical trials or to action research in a classroom, by connecting with those gathering and analysing social and environmental data, or by participating in new lines of dialogue and debate with leading thinkers in literature-based disciplines. The common ground across all disciplines is found in the benefits drawn from widening students' knowledge horizons and increasing their grasp of disciplinary depths, boundaries and bridges.

A particular benefit of connecting with researchers and research derives from the detailed awareness researchers have of what is *not* known. Faculty members at the University of Cambridge in the UK recently held a discussion about this, the notes from which offer the following insights:

> All the participants agreed strongly that there is value in having a researcher in the classroom. Paradoxically, participants agreed that the value of researchers is that they know what we don't know about the subject. A non-research-active teacher, or a textbook for that matter, can easily explain a subject and present a summary of knowledge that looks complete and authoritative. A researcher would unravel this knowledge, presenting a picture not just of what we know but also of what we don't know and of how people are trying to tackle the gaps in our knowledge.
>
> The researcher, that is, will be able to show students how knowledge is constructed in the discipline and will lecture in the penumbra of knowledge, exposing its outer limits. A teacher without research knowledge would struggle to do this, and it leads to a difference in focus in the classroom: non-researchers tell students what is known, researchers tell students what we don't know.
> (University of Cambridge; Personal email 21 October 2016.)

The principles of philosophical hermeneutics, as discussed in Chapter 1, find a strong echo here. We need to test interpretations of what we see and hear, and human knowledge must be underpinned by awareness of what is *not* known.

Learning, like research, is about paying attention to where the edges of knowledge are. This is at the core of scholarship: critiquing the potential weaknesses in the fabric of our existing knowledge, and seeking better knowledge and understanding.

Teaching-led research

It is worth also considering the potential of connecting students more readily with researchers and their work for the benefit of research. The primary focus in the field of research-based education tends to be on student learning, and the extent to which students benefit. But can researchers and research itself also benefit?

There is an emerging interest in this question. Tony Harland, Professor of Ecology at the University of Otago in New Zealand, draws on developments in his own curriculum to offer a conceptual argument for 'teaching-led research', in which 'university lecturers construct courses that directly and positively influence their research, while at the same time, safeguard and enhance the student experience' (Harland 2016, 461). He argues that teaching can be undertaken with a 'clear understanding that it enhances research' and that a 'research-pedagogy across the research-led higher education sector might be an attractive way for academics to go about their work, a caveat being that it must benefit both student and teacher'. Harland cites an empirical study by Robertson (2007), in which teachers in higher education reported that their teaching was, for them, a form of research and indivisible from it.

Recent work on 'Student as Producer' (Neary 2014, 28), developed at the University of Lincoln but now influencing a number of other institutions including some in the United States, presents a values-based, critical argument relating to the role of students in the academy:

> Student as Producer seeks to re-engineer the relationship between teaching and research to consolidate and restate the public values of academic life, emphasizing the role of students as collaborators with academics in the production and representation of knowledge and meaning. (Neary 2014)

The argument here is that students are capable of becoming co-producers of knowledge and of research 'outputs', and that recognising them as such can break down some of the orthodox hierarchies of the current higher education system. We will return to the potential of students creating research outputs when we look at the ways in which student assessments can be directed to specific audiences (Chapter 7).

6 Conclusions

The focus of this first dimension of the Connected Curriculum framework is both on enhancing student education and on promoting the importance of research. At their core, research-based education models, including the Connected Curriculum, are underpinned conceptually not only by social constructivist learning theories that highlight the need for active engagement in and ownership of one's own learning (Evans, Muijs and Tomlinson 2015), but also by a strong awareness of the need for *societies* to invest in research, and to be evidence-informed in their decision-making and practices. Research has been described in a recent

European policy paper as 'one of the best investments that can be made with public (and private) funds', with economic rates of return 'in the order of 20–50 per cent' (Georghiou 2015), and with significant additional benefits:

> the value of research is not only economic. There is a direct contribution to societal challenges (which itself requires better measurement through understanding impacts on human behaviour in general and on policy in particular). Beyond that research … should be valued for its role in creating a critical and reflexive society. (Georghiou 2015, 10)

Rather than setting the importance of research in opposition to that of student education, by seeing them as competing priorities, the challenge of developing the synergies between the two becomes the exciting goal.

7 Vignettes of practice

The following short case studies, or vignettes, highlight current practices across a range of university disciplines that reflect aspects of the first dimension of the Connected Curriculum framework. They illustrate some of the diverse ways in which it is possible for the principle 'students connect with research and researchers' to be put into practice.

The first vignette shows how a 'Meet the Professor' activity at UCL has been adapted and expanded to suit a range of science disciplines. The second presents a collaboration between two universities, one in Germany and one in the UK, which enables Archaeology students to experience research in another country, meeting with researchers both within and beyond their own institution. In the third, students in Ireland undertake summer projects in the social sciences, while in the fourth they engage with research-focused 3D modelling projects at the University of Reading. The fifth vignette addresses a common challenge associated with engaging students in research – that of giving them access to physical spaces and specialist equipment. It shows how the Open University in the UK is using virtual solutions to provide large numbers of students with access to research.

1. 'Meet the Professor' in Life and Medical Sciences at UCL

The aim of building the Meet the Professor activity in UCL Biosciences was to introduce our first-year students to the wide range of research activity undertaken in the department. While elements of current research are touched upon during year one lectures, we were aware that our new students did not have a clear perception of the extent and range of subjects that are under current investigation.

In 2012 we introduced a Meet the Professor session to our post-exam key skills timetable. This one-week, non-credit-bearing module was designed to expose our students to independent research as they design and follow a protocol to purify a specific protein. In addition, students consider future career options and work as a team, both in the laboratory and as part of a presentation team, and practice giving oral presentations. The Meet the Professor session complements this range of activities.

Students are sent to interview a member of the academic staff in groups. They are given the brief of finding out about their current research, their career path to date and any motivational people or events that influenced these choices. After the interview, students are asked to introduce 'their' academic to the rest of the student cohort via a short oral presentation, as dissemination of research knowledge is a key aim of this activity. Feedback from these sessions has been overwhelmingly positive, from both a staff and student perspective.

We have expanded its use in the first year of study so that students now have a similar experience looking at the work of their personal tutor. They begin by having an informal discussion in a scheduled tutorial meeting, then go away to carry out further independent research, which is presented as a single page report. After further discussion, students then visit the relevant research facilities within the department to further enhance their understanding of the research environment.

As a result of the success of this type of activity it has now been introduced to almost all of the personal tutorial systems on degree programmes within the Division of Biosciences, and implemented by other Faculties within the School of Life and Medical Sciences.

Vignette of practice submitted by Dr Amanda Cain, Senior Teaching Fellow and Deputy Head of Teaching for the UCL Molecular Biosciences degree, and Charmian Dawson, Teaching Fellow and PhD candidate.

2. Connecting Archaeology students with research across national borders: the *Q-Kolleg* at the Humboldt University, Berlin and the University of Nottingham, UK

In theory, Archaeology as a discipline offers plenty of opportunities for research-based education, for example in the form of hands-on engagement with ancient artefacts or through practical fieldwork campaigns. These have the potential to provide early experiences of working in international settings, and exposing students to different research methods and theoretical approaches. However, the extent to which this potential is harnessed varies considerably between different universities and curricula. The *Q-Kolleg* is an innovation that aims to provide sustainable opportunities for students to connect with research and researchers across national borders.

The *Q-Kolleg* started as a collaborative initiative linking the Winckelmann-Institute of Classical Archaeology at Humboldt-Universität zu Berlin (HU) with the Department of Classics at Nottingham University. Faculty members developed this format to expose students to different national traditions in their discipline. Under the general heading of 'Methods of studying images in Classical Archaeology', small groups of students (8–12; the 'Q-fellows') from both universities develop their own research projects around a predetermined case study. For example, students may investigate the friezes of the Pergamon altar in Berlin or of the Parthenon in London. Case studies run for an entire academic year.

To negotiate the geographical distance between the two groups, a blended learning approach is employed, whereby students collaborate as a plenary group in virtual milestone-conferences and participate in two *in situ* working visits. They meet in their local groups at HU and Nottingham and work independently in international HU-Nottingham pairs or small groups. Participating students gain not only research experience and disciplinary reflectivity but also language and intercultural competences.

The project begins with a virtual workshop, during which the two local groups are linked via video conferencing. During this session the students get to know each other and intensify their engagement with the initial theoretical and methodological input of senior academic staff at both institutions. The students form international pairs, based on shared tentative research interests, and begin independent work on developing a research question and project, with occasional feedback from the professors. These initial proposals are presented and discussed at a second virtual conference and reviewed thereafter. During a first week-long working visit at one of the two partner institutions, the students meet in person. Working hands-on, they are coached on objects and texts related to their projects, participate in research seminars and present their work-in-progress. After this, students continue to work in pairs on their project, contextualise their findings and submit drafts of their project reports for peer review online. The *Q-Kolleg* concludes with a second week-long visit to the other institution, with an emphasis on reflecting on the research process and preparing the finished work for presentations at the host institution.

The *Q-Kolleg* in Archaeology/Classics has run five times since autumn 2012. After successful evaluation, adapted versions have run in the Departments of German Literature (collaboration with Columbia University, New York), Cultural Studies (with the Universidad Naçional de Colombia, Bogotá), Art History (with the University of Innsbruck) and Economics (with the National University of Singapore).

Vignette of practice submitted by Wolfgang Deicke, who leads the bologna.lab at HU in Berlin, a cross-faculty laboratory for the development and implementation of innovative teaching and learning formats, and Arne Reinhardt, formerly a research associate in the Winckelmann-Institute of HU and leader of the Q-Kolleg in Classical Archaeology, now at the Institute of Classical Archaeology at the University of Heidelberg.

3. Research Summer School at the Royal College of Surgeons in Ireland

The Research Summer School (RSS) has created a space that provides a stimulus for all our undergraduate students from the Schools of Medicine, Pharmacy and Physiotherapy. It empowers them to start their transition to be our researchers of the future.

Students seek out their own research project and apply for funding from internal and external sources. This gives them an insight into the highly competitive environment of research. Once they have secured their research project they participate in the RSS programme. This runs for eight weeks during the summer. It commences with Research Skills Workshops, which are delivered to all students over the first two days. The intention is to give our students their 'tool box' as they set out on their research journey for the summer. It includes a series of talks and hands-on activities. Topics covered include Clinical Study Design, Research Governance, Drug Targeting, Nanomedicine and Analysis of Genetic Material.

(Continued)

The programme continues with the Friday Discovery Series, whereby students interact directly with researchers from the research community. Each researcher delivers an interactive session with the intention of exposing the students to aspects of research where they can hone their analytical and critical skills. An integral aspect of the programme is the Book Club, which allows students to interface with the Humanities. Each student is gifted a copy of the book of choice which is contextual and intentionally provocative. Their remit is to read the book in time for a discussion session with in-house researchers.

Students are required to submit an abstract, poster and slide presentation of their summer research for participation in the annual RCSI Research Day. They are encouraged to submit their work to conferences and for publication. The RSS has also empowered our students to create their own Research Conference: ICHAMS (International Conference for Healthcare and Medical Students; www.ichams.org), now in its fifth year. The concept of the RSS is intentionally flexible, providing a springboard for students to create opportunities that allow them to become more intimately involved in research.

Students benefit by taking active responsibility and ownership of their learning in their own research projects. They manage their experiences proactively, independently constructing their own knowledge. Putting the research they undertake into the context of their studies more widely, they can make connections between different elements of their learning and come to recognise the beauty in the persistence of becoming an expert.

Submitted by Dr Sarah O'Neill, Director of the Royal College of Surgeons in Ireland Research Summer School (RSS) and Senior Lecturer in the Department of Molecular and Cellular Therapeutics.

4. Classics and 3D digital modelling at the University of Reading

3D digital modelling offers a powerful way of visualising vanished buildings and places. A large digital model of ancient Rome created by a researcher, Dr Matthew Nicholls, proved popular with students, who often asked about the research and modelling process underlying the final, visual results. A scheme was developed, funded through the University of Reading's Undergraduate Research Opportunities Programme, to establish the potential for working with students as research partners and for teaching them the necessary software competence.

This series of pilots, which also involved talking to software experts and other 3D educators worldwide, worked well. Undergraduate-researched 3D reconstructions, for example, were broadcast in a BBC TV documentary on Roman Scotland, with the student researcher named in the programme credits.

Dr Nicholls then developed an undergraduate module in which students learn to use simple but powerful 3D modelling software (called SketchUp) to create reconstructions of buildings from the nearby Roman town of Silchester. This connects to the University of Reading's own extensive excavation work and field school at the site. The module encourages the development of advanced computing skills that are unusual within the context of a UK humanities degree, and which have proved useful to more than one student in subsequent job interviews.

Although this module is radically different in its content and assessment from others offered by the Classics department, its leader worked with external examiners and colleagues across the University to ensure parity of intellectual depth and rigour by requiring, for example, a written commentary to accompany the digital work, explaining the aims of each student's model and the choices made in its construction.

The resulting module has proved popular with students and has gathered substantial attention within and beyond the University: this work led to Dr Nicholls winning the national Guardian/Higher Education Academy Teaching Excellence Award in 2014. This educational work also contributes to Dr Nicholls' academic 'outputs': he regularly uses his own digital models in commercial, broadcast, and public-facing contexts.

Case study submitted Dr Matthew Nicholls, Associate Professor and Roman historian in the Classics Department of the University of Reading.

5. Access to research through the virtual world at the Open University

The Open Science Laboratory at the Open University in the UK is an online laboratory that brings practical experimental science to students wherever they are. The laboratory uses a mixture of experiments and investigations based on on-screen instruments, remote-access experiments and virtual scenarios using real data.

(Continued)

A number of the activities are available to everyone, while others are available only to students of the Open University.

A key principle is that all the science is authentic. Interactive screen experiments capture every step of a real experiment conducted in a physical laboratory and then allow the remote user to follow a 'virtual' (but not simulated) version of the experiment. Others simulate exact conditions – for example, one field trip allows geological fieldwork to be conducted in a 3D immersive environment.

There are also remote experiments. For example, PIRATE is a remote-controlled observatory with a 17-inch telescope on a robotic mount. Students and researchers are able to book times when they are able to control the telescope to collect their own data (http://pirate.open.ac.uk).

The laboratory has a number of tools for helping students create, conduct and manage their research investigations. Many of the activities are embedded within the Open University curriculum but they also exist as standalone activities. In addition, increasing use is made of webcasting technology to stream live experiments being conducted in the lab and allow students to influence the decisions taken about the way in which the experiments are conducted.

Vignette of practice submitted by Dr Sam Smidt, formerly Director of Student Learning Experience and Associate Dean (Learning and Teaching) in the Faculty of Science at the Open University, now Principal Teaching Fellow in the UCL Arena Centre for Research-based Education.

4

Connected programme design

Introduction

The second dimension of the Connected Curriculum framework, 'A throughline of research activity is built into each programme', has three related strands, each of which depends on coherent programme design:

- creating a related sequence of opportunities for research and enquiry, so that students steadily build up their abilities and confidence;
- prompting students to make conceptual connections between apparently disparate elements of their wider programme;
- enabling students to develop a clear picture, or narrative, of their overall learning journey and to analyse their personal progress and future goals.

The contention is that a well designed mandatory sequence of core activities, for all students studying on a particular programme (that is, studying for the same academic award), can achieve all three of these challenges simultaneously, such that they reinforce each other. In this chapter we consider different ways in which this might be achieved and then look more closely at why 'joined up' programme design is important for students. We conclude with four vignettes of current practice.

Practical approaches to creating a connected 'throughline' of enquiry

Ensuring that programmes of study are designed coherently can be a challenge, especially for institutions that use modularised systems in which students studying for the same degree can make very different study choices from those of their peers on the same programme. Some programmes build in a very high degree of student choice, while others are made up predominantly of compulsory topics of study. Even in the latter, it is not always straightforward to build students' skills in research and enquiry incrementally through the length of the programme, or to enable students to see how the different areas of knowledge and skills covered by the programme relate to one another. Neither is it easy for students to gain a clear overview of their own knowledge, skills and values as these develop during their period of study.

Building a core sequence of enquiry-based learning opportunities has great promise. It can even lead to a programme-wide Showcase Portfolio, allowing students to collate and curate their best work for assessment. But what might all this look like in practice? The following ten approaches are neither exhaustive nor mutually exclusive but illustrate possibilities from which programme leaders and teams can select, or which may stimulate other effective ideas.

1. **Creating a sequence of mandatory modules**, which clearly follow on through each year (or phase) of study and which explicitly challenge students to build their own connected learning narrative. This may be achieved, for example, by:
   - foregrounding the principles and practices of active research and enquiry in the core modules (this should be a principle for any fully 'connected curriculum', as the key is empowering students to undertake research and enquiry increasingly through their programme);
   - building on a core conceptual theme, such as ethical practice, global citizenship or sustainability, which acts as a vehicle for enabling students to make connections between the broader spectrum of topics that make up the whole programme;
   - foregrounding the core principles of practice in the discipline, e.g. 'Becoming a historian', 'Becoming a physicist', or 'Professionalism in Architecture'.

2. **Creating a series of 'Connections' modules**, which act like the mandatory, connective modules above but allow for some student choice. For example, in year one there could be two Connections modules and students choose only one. Both modules would require links across different ideas/topics to be made but each would

orientate around different knowledge content. Ideally there should be new subject content for the students in these modules; the new material can then act as a springboard for challenging students to connect the new insights with other themes covered on the programme.

3. **Creating a single linear module that stretches from the beginning to the end** of the programme, running alongside other optional modules. Such a module would include a sequence of assessment points that collectively anchor core learning and the development of skills needed for research and enquiry. This can be a challenge for regulations orientated around formally completing credits at each level but these may be overcome by setting assessment points that need simply to be completed at each stage but which can be revisited, improved and formally assessed later. One possibility for such a degree-long module is to design it fluidly, so that students must undertake tasks but are working towards a Showcase Portfolio in which they select their best 'outputs' for final, summative submission. They can be asked to include in the portfolio, where useful, analytical reflections on their own learning: their own learning story. The Showcase Portfolio (see Chapter 7) has the advantage of enabling students to take risks without penalty; if they have tried something but not fully succeeded, they can explain in the final portfolio what they learned from that experience.

4. **Building timetabled peer study groups into the full length of the degree.** In these groups, students are challenged to work together to make, work on and report on conceptual or professional themes to the wider cohort. They may do this, for example, via an online discussion forum, blog or co-created wiki. These activities can feed into formative or, preferably, summative assessments; if students receive marks, they may be more motivated to engage. Decisions need to be made about where group marks should count and where individual marks should be taken into consideration; a balance of the two is often preferable. Students' abilities to articulate conceptual and professional connections across apparently disparate topics can be rewarded highly, and emphasised in the assessment criteria.

5. **Orientating the whole degree programme towards a real-world event**, such as an undergraduate or postgraduate research

conference. The theme of research and enquiry can be flagged as central to the shape of the degree, and the whole programme shaped so that it culminates in an undergraduate conference. Planning such a conference can involve a whole suite of challenges, including working with alumni and/or employers to shape the event, as well as speaking at and critiquing one another during the conference itself.

6. **Designing a 'capstone' module** for the final year/learning phase (e.g. in the last term or semester) in which students are explicitly challenged to draw on and apply learning from across all dimensions of their studies to a complex, multi-faceted task, problem or challenge.

7. **Creating a single core assessment** – for example, a reflectively analytical portfolio – that builds from phase to phase. This may be built into a sequence of connective modules (1 and 2), assessed alongside a capstone module (6) or overseen in academic tutorials (10). Formative feedback from assessors along the way helps to shape students' development and improve the work as they progress.

8. **Using a programme of online learning** which runs in parallel with face-to-face elements, but which provides structured opportunities for students to make connections between the full spectrum of topics. Online tutorial support and/or peer engagement add value here.

9. **Ensuring that connective themes are regularly revisited as a repeated motif in the content and student assessments.** This can be a means of enhancing a programme in which modules (or sub-units) are entirely or predominantly mandatory, a common situation for programmes accredited by external professional bodies. In this case, there may still be opportunities to build in some of the other features listed here, if suitable for the context.

10. **Underpinning the programme with an academic tutorial system**, in which students work in small groups with the support of a tutor to connect and interrogate aspects of their learning. Tutors can meet with tutor groups and use guided conversations, for example, to encourage students to reflect on their overall understandings of the discipline, the various ways in which investigations are carried out within it, and the extent to which students feel confident that they are developing the skills needed to succeed on their programme of study.

3 Undergraduate and postgraduate programmes: similarities and differences

The above features of curriculum design are just indicative of many possibilities. Choices made are likely to be affected by what have been described as the 'signature pedagogies' (Shulman 2005) of the given discipline. Decisions about curriculum design will also depend on the length and level of the degree programme; these differ most obviously between undergraduate and postgraduate awards.

For undergraduate programmes, which may be from three to six years in duration, there are various creative possibilities in terms of the use of mandatory and optional modules, and how to map content, learning activities and assessments not only across a given year of study but also across the years. For taught postgraduate programmes, there will be fewer design options available but still perhaps more flexibility than some institutions and departments have taken up. How might a Masters degree become more effectively 'connected'?

In the UK, a Masters programme is typically worth 180 credits. These are often made up of 120 learning credits, divided into taught modules, which often include some optionality for students, followed by 60 credits allocated to an independent research project. Because postgraduate programmes may only last for one year, there is particular benefit in designing the curriculum very carefully to make sure that students negotiate the transition into postgraduate study quickly and become fully prepared to undertake the research study needed in the final year phase.

This preparation often takes the form of a designated module about research, for example introducing methodologies, methods and ethics, and/or embedding aspects of these topics into the wider module choices. As with undergraduate programmes, it may be useful and possible to create a linear module that lasts the full length of the period of study, for which students experience a combination of peer and tutor support. Such a module can both introduce approaches to research and support the student through their choices of research project. It can even make use of the Showcase Portfolio approach (Chapter 7), inviting students to collate and/or curate their best work, including their research dissertation, and to present it as a whole.

Similar functions can be carried out in an academic tutor group, which can offer some individualised support and guidance as well as challenging students in groups to deepen their levels of overall understanding and extend their intellectual and practical skills. The number of students in a cohort and ratio of students to teachers will help determine what is practical.

4 Key questions for departments and programme teams

The key questions for departments, programme leaders and teaching teams to consider include:

1. When and how are we empowering students to make explicit connections between apparently disparate elements of the programme(s)?
2. How are we ensuring that students build steadily their capacity for collaborative and independent research and enquiry, and that they are able to describe these research-related skills?
3. With the above questions in mind, are we happy with the relationship of modules or sub-units to one another in terms of degree of difficulty and centrality to the programme aims?
4. Are we assessing students' learning in such a way that aspects of their personal learning story, as well as the different elements of their learning, are captured?
5. Are we content that core modules, if not all modules, situate the students, whether in small groups or as individuals, as active, critical learners?
6. Does the progression of student assessments, in terms of the content of what is being assessed, look 'joined up'?
7. Do the types of assessment across the programme (e.g. essays, group projects, video documentaries, presentations, responding to a design brief) link logically together, testing a range of skills?
8. Is the pattern and timing of assessments such that students can receive constructive feedback on formative activities before being formally (summatively) tested to allocate marks or grades?
9. Has the programme team agreed on an appropriate range of feedback methods (e.g. personalised written feedback; online group feedback that synthesises key learning points for the whole cohort; face-to-face feedback in small tutorials, tutors' 'office hours', or seminars)?
10. Has the programme team decided how to communicate these feedback methods clearly to students, so that they understand fully that they are vital opportunities for feedback that will feed into their future learning? If necessary, are students asked to refer

to and use that feedback explicitly, for example by synthesising key learning points in an academic tutorial or on the cover sheet of the next assignment?

11. Is the overall balance of mandatory and optional modules right for the discipline and context?
12. Looking at the design of the programme as a whole, is there a clear rationale for the structure in terms of increasing the levels of difficulty through the phases of the programme?

The invitation to use the above questions assumes that all members of a programme team – those who contribute to the teaching and assessment on that degree – recognise the importance of seeing the programme as a whole, rather than just seeing it as a set of loosely connected units of study. The institution has a role to play here in creating spaces for collective planning and promoting a shared sense of responsibility. Knowing why it is helpful for students to make connections across the elements of their study can be helpful and we turn here to underpinning theory.

5 Learning as a coherent personal narrative of enquiry

This dimension's focus on *enquiry* as an integral part of curriculum design is not just about building enquiry-based learning opportunities through the length and structure of the programme, although this is important; it is also about empowering students to use enquiry to develop their own coherent story of who they are, what they can do and where they want to go. Each student comes into higher education with her or his own personal story. Characteristics such as educational background, nationality, ethnicity, religion, class, gender, sexual orientation, accessibility needs, age and current personal circumstances will differ: each has a unique personal story and identity that needs to be respected. To become educated is not just to know more; it is about confidently being who you are, and taking ownership of the ways in which you are changing as a person through intellectual critique and interpersonal engagement.

A great deal has been said and written about 'student experience' in recent years, much of it conflated with ideas of 'customer experience' rather than about how students encounter learning and enquiry as part of their wider lived experience. The second dimension of the

Connected Curriculum framework, 'A throughline of research activity is built into each programme', directs our attention not only to the overall shape and structure of the whole programme of study and the impact of its design upon students' learning but also to the extent to which they experience a coherent developmental journey of discovery that is *meaningful* to them. If we see education as a form of moving towards a new picture of oneself through critical dialogue with others, it is inherently about developing one's own identity, voice and story.

There has been a growing interest in the importance of narrative to education in recent decades, both as a research methodology and as a means of making sense of complex human experience over time. Jerome Bruner, a leading psychologist and educationist of the twentieth century, observes that the term derives from the verb 'to tell' (*narrare*) and also from a noun meaning 'knowing in some particular way' (*gnarus*). He describes a neurological disorder called *dysnarrativia*, a severe impairment in the ability to understand stories (2002, 86, 89). This impairment prevents our being able to make sense of ourselves, because narratives:

> impose a structure, a compelling reality on what we experience, even a philosophical stance.

Narratives allow us to look backwards and forwards, as well as interpreting the present; they enable us to make sense of our experience over periods of time (Bruner 2002; Clandinin 2000; Clough 2002; Erben 2000). And narrative is not just about the experience of one individual; it enables us to express our engagement with others through our uniquely human 'capacity for intersubjectivity', which is 'a precondition for our collective life in culture' (Bruner 2002, 16). Gadamer's 'merging of horizons', in the tradition of philosophical hermeneutics, finds an echo here once again.

Each student who comes to study in higher education is also coming into a new sense of self: our personal identities are changed when we study and these changes may be particularly significant to those for whom coming to higher level study is not the norm in their culture, class or local peer group (Fung 2007). Bruner notes that:

> there is no such thing as an intuitively obvious and essential self to know, one that just sits there ready to be portrayed in words. Rather we constantly construct and reconstruct our selves... Telling oneself about oneself is like making up a story about who and what

we are, what's happened, and why we're doing what we're doing. (Bruner 2002, 64)

Narrative is particularly effective for capturing change over a period of time, and learning always involves change. Michael Erben (2000), drawing on Bruner's work, argues that:

> it is narrative that provides the cohering mechanism to make such experience comprehensible. (Erben 2000, 383)

An advantage of narrative as a form of knowing is that 'it does not regard lives (or the interpretation of lives) as collections of segmented events' (Erben 2000, 383). It is common in higher education for 'student experience' to be measured through surveys, and also common for students' learning to be tested in examinations at given moments in time. These instruments take a snapshot, gleaning information about particular aspects of experience or insights into knowledge of a particular field at a given moment. Both have their uses. But through developing a more holistic learning narrative, students can construct a more nuanced picture of their emerging sense of who they are and of how they relate to their discipline(s) and the world around them:

> A self-making narrative is something of a balancing act. It must, on the one hand, create a conviction of autonomy, that one has a will of one's own, a certain freedom of choice, a degree of possibility. But it must also relate the self to a world of others – to friends and family, to institutions, to the past, to reference groups. (Bruner 2002, 78)

The second dimension of the Connected Curriculum, then, is intended to highlight the importance of students' developing a coherent learning narrative.

A learning narrative can simply be an internalised, personal account. But it can be explicitly expressed to others via work produced by the students. This might be through a sequence of separate but conceptually related student assessments that communicate current learning to others. Students' learning narratives can also, where appropriate for the discipline, be developed more holistically, for example via a continuous portfolio (or Showcase Portfolio) of 'outputs' or 'products' that have narrative qualities, and/or through a narrative 'wrapper' in which students explicitly analyse some of the key relationships between different elements of the work they have produced. This is already familiar territory in many professional degree programmes such as medicine and education; it is less common in disciplines that are not accredited in line with the standards of a given profession. Yet this approach may be just as useful for all students, especially where they are often learning through active research and/or enquiry, where they are engaging with more than one, narrowly framed discipline, and where they are learning beyond as well as within the formal curriculum, for example when taking up work placements or studying abroad. Developing a personal learning narrative as part of a programme-wide portfolio, in whatever form, can also help students articulate their knowledge, skills and achievements to prospective employers (Chapter 5).

In what forms *might* such a connective narrative be expressed? This is likely to vary across disciplines. The sense of a student's unfolding learning story may be captured indirectly through written text which is relatively impersonal, for example in the form of an analytical 'metastudy' of a sequence of related topics. It can alternatively be conveyed through a more personal reflective journal with analytic qualities or through a holistic professional or creative portfolio. With the use of accessible new technologies, it can also be expressed through more visual means such as storyboards, blogs or film documentaries. Whatever the form of communication, a student's personal story may also be co-created, at least in part, for example with peers, researchers, practitioners or technical specialists. We will consider more of the possibilities afforded by student assessments in Chapter 7.

6 Vignettes of practice

Creating a connected 'throughline' of research and enquiry and thus enabling students to own and create their own learning narrative is a complex but rewarding design challenge. There is no simple 'quick fix' for this but there is a spectrum of possibilities for programme teams to consider.

The following vignettes of practice highlight the diversity of possible ways of enabling students to make conceptual connections across different topics, modules and/or investigative projects. The first is an example of a Showcase Portfolio from the University of Sydney, in which students select their best work over a period of time to exemplify their insights and skills. The second shows how at UCL one discipline has designed its modular undergraduate programmes to include a connected sequence of core modules, which support the development of a fieldwork portfolio and a critical blog addressing global issues. The third illustrates the use by another UCL discipline of a personal tutoring programme that challenges students to make connections between different elements of their learning across all three years of study, and the fourth vignette illustrates a co-curricular approach to the development of a connected professional development e-portfolio at the University College Dublin Medical School.

1. Holistic portfolio for health professional students at the University of Sydney, Australia

This portfolio for health professional students studying medical imaging at postgraduate level asks them to collect one medical image of particular significance to them, every week across their two-year programme. They are asked to research the anatomy/pathology identified in the image and write half a referenced page of explanation/reflection. For example, they might analyse whether the image represents a typical or an atypical finding for that particular anatomy/pathology.

It is crucial to provide initial structured support and this is done through a dedicated portfolio tutorial in which students work on a scenario-based example, from which they create their own exemplar, with class-based discussion and feedback. The students' portfolios start with simple accomplishments early in the programme and build in complexity as their experience and confidence grows. Towards the end of their programme, they have almost 100 entries from which to curate a showcase portfolio evidencing their level of expertise across the domains required for professional accreditation.

Introduced to encourage the kind of learning they would need *beyond* the course as they move from competence to expertise, the importance of the portfolio to students *during* their course is that both clinical supervisors and academic staff alike can simply and rapidly appreciate (and assess) the level of progress the student has made and provide necessary assistance and/or challenges where needed. And *after* qualification they have developed a routine for evidence-based practice and continuing learning. The portfolio thus serves both formative and summative purposes during the course, is used as a showcase portfolio at the end of the course and, importantly, influences future learning in professional practice.

Vignette of practice submitted by Dr Jillian Clarke, Senior Lecturer, Discipline of Medical Radiation Sciences, Faculty of Health Sciences, University of Sydney, Australia.

2. Designing a research throughline in undergraduate Archaeology degrees at UCL, UK

The undergraduate programmes for Archaeology students at UCL are deliberately structured around a sequence of compulsory modules, each focused on different aspects of research and skills training. These culminate in a large, final year research dissertation. In the first year of study, students take 'Introduction to Archaeology' and 'Field Methods' and in the second year they focus on 'Interpreting Evidence' and 'Research and Presentation Skills'.

Students also take, in parallel, a set of compulsory modules connected by a common theme, that of global citizenship. These modules focus on world archaeology, archaeological theory and public archaeology. All students undertake at least 70 days of archaeological fieldwork, museum placement or public engagement in diverse locations around the world. Some students also elect to participate in UCL's Global Citizenship programme, a two-week summer project in which students from different disciplines meet to address a complex global challenge (https://www.ucl.ac.uk/global-citizenship/programme).

The structured progression of linked activities through the undergraduate Archaeology degrees equips students to complete a critical fieldwork portfolio and also to create a blog in which they discuss the relevance of archaeology to major issues of public debate. Alongside the mandatory 'throughline' modules, students take a number of optional modules so that they can shape, customise and extend their own learning. Towards the end of their second year, students identify their final-year dissertation topic and are given supervisorial support to undertake original research. This is discussed through an oral presentation prior to the submission of a 10,000 word thesis.

Vignette of practice submitted by Professor Sue Hamilton, Professor of Prehistory and Director of the UCL Institute of Archaeology and Dr Bill Sillar, Chair of the Institute of Archaeology Teaching Committee.

3. Personal tutoring to facilitate connected learning on the BA Education Studies programme at the UCL Institute of Education, UK

This Personal Tutoring Programme at the Institute of Education has two main aims. First, the personal tutor works with students throughout their degree to help them to produce a narrative portfolio. Second, the personal tutor helps to guide their students' overall academic progress, supporting their personal and professional well-being and development during their studies.

Every student on the BA Education Studies degree is assigned a personal tutor at the beginning of their first year of study, who works with them through the entire three years of their degree. Each personal tutor works with a group of about 10–12 students in a given year of study. Students typically meet with their personal tutor at least six times over the year, towards the beginning and end of each term. Some of these opportunities to meet might be group meetings with the other students who are part of their personal tutor group and some will be individual meetings with their personal tutor.

On the BA Education Studies, we believe that students should be able to graduate with more than just a number. They should be able to leave with a detailed narrative account that describes the actual work that they have been doing during the three years: this is the narrative portfolio. Every student's portfolio will be unique and the product of the work that they do with their personal tutor. The kinds of things that their portfolio will document might include: their own learning goals and approaches; the specific issues, theories and concerns that motivate their work; the specific topics and debates that they have worked on in their module assignments; the links that they have made between their different modules; and the connections they have made between their modules and other areas of their work, public, community and family life.

A narrative portfolio has many uses. For example, it can help both the students and their personal tutors make informed decisions about the best module options for them, about the best essay topics to work on within their modules, and about dissertation topics. Toward the end of their time on the programme, it can help the student and tutor put together detailed letters of recommendation, letters of application and personal CVs to send on to employers or postgraduate programmes. Throughout the students' time on their course and beyond, their narrative portfolio can help demonstrate both to them and to others that the work they do at university has far more richness and meaning than could ever possibly be measured in one single numerical mark.

Vignette submitted by Stuart Tannock, Programme Leader, BA Education Studies at UCL Institute of Education.

4. Medical Professionalism in Research and Education at University College Dublin (UCD), Republic of Ireland

In the UCD School of Medicine a new 'connected curriculum' initiative is under development. Entitled *Medical Professionalism in Research and Education* (MPRE), it will run in the co-curricular space for the duration of the medical degree programme. By using digital badging as a reward mechanism, students will be incentivised to take ownership of their learning journey through the programme and onwards into the Continuing Professional Development (CPD) space.

By means of a reflective e-portfolio, students will be guided through four digital badging levels (bronze, silver, gold and platinum), which will encourage and prompt students to invest in learning opportunities. Students will be rewarded for engaging in relevant co-curricular activities, research modules will be available as electives and, as the student progresses through the curriculum, they will also be rewarded for mentoring other students who are beginning on their learning journey. Each of the digital badging levels have various criteria attached, which the students can engage with and then reflect on their activities in their e-portfolio. The intention is that, by the end of their time in Medical School, students will have a comprehensive portfolio of their professional activities in research and education. They will then continue with this reflective practice as medical practitioners. The ultimate aim of MPRE is to foster and promote the continuous learning cycle in medicine of observation, participation and demonstration that occurs throughout a medical career.

Submitted by Dr Cliona McGovern, Assistant Professor, Forensic & Legal Medicine, School of Medicine, University College Dublin, Republic of Ireland.

5

Connecting across disciplines and out to the world

Introduction

The third dimension of the Connected Curriculum framework, 'Students make connections across subjects and out to the world', highlights the importance of students having opportunities to make conceptual connections between their own subject(s) and other disciplines. They may be able to study with students and faculty members from outside their main subject field and have opportunities to look outwards to the world; that is, they become aware of some of our complex global challenges. In doing this, they can be empowered to consider their own values and future contribution to the world. They can also engage with international perspectives, developing their awareness of knowledge traditions from cultures that differ from their own.

As highlighted in Chapter 2, the disciplinary cultures and structures of our higher education institutions continue to have a strong impact on the ways in which students study and on what they study. In recent years, however, there has been increased interest in interdisciplinary ways of working. Literature suggests that while specialist expertise remains vital, there is a growing need to prepare students for crosscutting forms of enquiry in a world where challenges are so complex and yet so profoundly interconnected (British Academy 2016; Lyall et al. 2016). Where different areas of knowledge have become sharply differentiated within universities, forming themselves into distinctive disciplines with firm boundaries, opportunities may be lost to develop new theoretical framings, new ways of gathering and analysing evidence and new possibilities for society.

How might institutions and departments tackle the challenge of making the most of interdisciplinary possibilities, while sustaining excellence within disciplinary specialisms? We look here at some practical ways of developing interdisciplinary and cross-disciplinary learning opportunities for students, starting with making modest adjustments to existing programmes and then looking at some more radical approaches. We go on to explore some of the theory behind interdisciplinary approaches, and conclude with some vignettes of practice reflecting this dimension of the Connected Curriculum framework.

2 Enriching current programmes through connecting with other disciplines

Students choosing to study in higher education often, but not always, select a single or at least a main (major) discipline for specialist study before they begin their degree. There are significant variations in the way this plays out across the sector internationally, however. In some national and/or institutional contexts, students typically experience a broad selection of topics for study on arrival at university and only specialise in later years of study. On distance learning programmes, too, there may be wide flexibility in choosing topics to make up a degree award. But on more traditional degree programmes, and in the UK in particular, students typically select a main or even single subject of study – for example English, Mathematics or Physics – before they step across the campus threshold, and their focus may be very much on that subject throughout their studies.

Of course some 'disciplines' are intrinsically multi-disciplinary and perhaps more accurately described as fields. Subjects such as Archaeology and Geography are made up of a number of elements, crossing from the physical sciences through the social sciences to the humanities. And those that are professionally accredited, leading towards a specific professional qualification, have their own characteristics. These subjects – for example, Medicine, Architecture and Education – draw from a range of 'pure' and applied disciplines but are very carefully and holistically designed to ensure that graduates are thoroughly prepared for the given profession. Postgraduate degrees also vary considerably: some are very specifically focused on one specialism, while others pull together a number of subjects and offer significant flexibility.

These variations in context mean that the third dimension of the Connected Curriculum offers a different kind of challenge to each of these different contexts. For programmes of study that already comprise different disciplinary perspectives, the challenge is one of considering whether these can be enhanced. Do the kinds of connective curriculum features described in Chapter 4 afford new possibilities? Could aspects of the connected 'throughline' of enquiry, such as academic tutorials, a capstone module or a Showcase Portfolio provide new ways of stretching students, challenging them to analyse links and contrasts between different disciplinary perspectives and methods?

Some students are in effect 'visiting' other disciplines, for example by taking on an optional module or project from another. Others may be studying two disciplines in parallel, as is commonplace in 'combined honours' programmes in the UK. One or more of these connective design features may be employed to empower students to make stronger intellectual connections between fields, and to be rewarded for doing so.

For programmes comprising a single discipline, discussion may more usefully focus on whether and where there could be opportunities for students to take a wider view. Can curriculum features described in the last chapter, such as Connections modules, afford new possibilities for students to step beyond their main area of study as they undertake research and enquiry? Even tightly knit disciplines can offer opportunities for students to range beyond the home subject, so that they can come back to it with fresh eyes.

3 Developing new interdisciplinary programmes

A more radical way of enabling students to connect across disciplines is to offer fully integrated, interdisciplinary programmes. These are more common for Masters degrees but also possible at undergraduate level. We look here at two programmes at UCL whose development was underway before the Connected Curriculum initiative was introduced but which illustrate many of its characteristics: the Bachelor of Arts and Sciences (BASc) degree and the Integrated Engineering Programme (IEP).

Bachelors of Arts and Sciences

The first innovative example of an interdisciplinary programme of study is that of the Bachelor of Arts and Sciences (BASc) degree at UCL (UCL

2016k). The director of this degree, Carl Gombrich, has outlined the thinking behind its introduction (British Academy 2016, 71–78). He defines an interdisciplinary degree as one in which:

- students study in more than one academic department;
- students study some courses that are explicitly inter-/cross-/post-disciplinary;
- students are asked explicitly (by means of a dissertation or other work) to synthesize or contrast the knowledge acquired in more than one discipline.

Gombrich notes that, although a number of students in the UK and beyond do study more than one subject as part of their degree, it is less common for them to be asked explicitly to make connections between its different elements. The BASc takes a distinctive stand in doing this, by requiring students both to study across the sciences and the arts, humanities and social sciences *and* to undertake 'some synthesizing of disciplinary perspectives' (Gombrich, in British Academy 2016, 73).

Students on the programme follow one of four disciplinary Pathways:

- Cultures (Humanities and Arts)
- Societies (Social Sciences, Law)
- Health and Environment (Health and Environmental Sciences)
- Sciences and Engineering (Hard Sciences, Maths and Computer Sciences)

Reflecting the idea of a connective core or throughline of enquiry, the BASc requires students to engage with a number of core courses (Table 5.1), alongside a range of options. The core courses include modules in which students explicitly engage with areas of thought and study in ways that cut across typical university subject boundaries.

Topics such as Approaches to Knowledge, Qualitative Thinking and Object-based Learning (Chatterjee and Hannan 2015) shine very specific lights on the contrasts between different ways of undertaking enquiry. They also afford opportunities for making and critiquing connections across disciplines and of linking those connections with 'real world' challenges.

The BASc programme is extremely popular, with high numbers of students applying to it, very good student evaluations and very strong graduate employment. Its connective features may stimulate thinking for leaders of other kinds of programmes.

Table 5.1 Bachelor of Arts and Sciences (BASc) Core Modules (2016/2017)

Phases of study	Core Modules
Year One	• Approaches to Knowledge: Introduction to Interdisciplinarity • Interdisciplinary Research Methods • Quantitative Methods and Mathematical Thinking • Language • End-of-year Lab Conference
Year Two	• Object lessons: Communicating Knowledge through Collections • Quantitative Methods 2: Data Science and Visualisation • Making Value Judgements: Qualitative Thinking • Interdisciplinary Elective • Language
Summer at end of Year Two	• Internship
Year Three (Y001 Only)	• Year Abroad at an approved university • Study Abroad Dissertation
Final Year	• The Knowledge Economy • Dissertation • Language

An interdisciplinary professional programme: the Integrated Engineering Programme

The second example of an interdisciplinary undergraduate degree is the Integrated Engineering Programme (IEP) at UCL. This programme aims to combine innovative teaching methods and an industry-oriented curriculum with discipline-specific, accredited degree programmes. Participating throughout the degree in interdisciplinary activities, students develop their transferable professional skills in the context of real-world engineering projects (UCL 2016m).

Bains et al. (2015) explain that the IEP draws on the Connected Curriculum philosophy by tapping into the institution's research-base:

It is founded on the premise that although a strong disciplinary engineering foundation is vital, modern engineering problems do not respect these disciplinary boundaries. This means that students have to learn to work in multi-disciplinary teams on interdisciplinary problems.

Although engineering specialisms are maintained, a series of crosscutting activities enables students to collaborate to solve complex problems and challenges (Figure 5.1).

The programme's core modules enable students to develop engineering modelling, design and analysis skills, in addition to professional and transferable skills. Key to its design is enabling students to appreciate the interdisciplinary nature of Engineering as a field; students start to work in interdisciplinary teams in their very first term and continue to work on challenges and scenarios through the programme. They are also able to undertake a major interdisciplinary capstone project. As students progress through the programme, they have opportunities to see and engage with relevant research activities in the department and beyond.

These two programmes illustrate ways of bringing disciplines together through designing a whole new programme and using interdisciplinary connections as an underpinning characteristic. Specialist, single-disciplinary programmes of study are likely to want to make much more modest enhancements to their programme when reflecting on the benefits to students of stepping outside their home subject at some point during their studies. However, this dimension of the Connected Curriculum aims to prompt all programme teams to take a fresh look at the opportunities currently provided and consider whether they can be strengthened meaningfully within the local context.

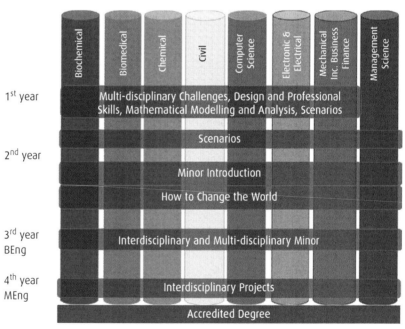

Fig. 5.1   Structure of the UCL Integrated Engineering Programme

4 Why is connecting across disciplines important?

University disciplines and their cultures

The history of academic disciplines is a long and curious one. The writer and physicist C. P. Snow wrote with regret, in the aftermath of World War Two, of the emergence in the twentieth century of 'two cultures': 'literary intellectuals' and 'scientists' (Snow 1959). Snow, for whom this polarisation is 'a sheer loss to us all' (1959, 12), railed against the inability of literary intellectuals (those in the arts, humanities and social sciences) to engage in any serious way with science. They in turn critiqued scientists for not educating themselves in literary culture:

> There seems to be no place where the [disciplinary] cultures meet. I am not going to waste time saying that this is a pity. It is much worse than that.

Snow argued that 'creative chances' should result from the 'clashing point' of disciplines as they meet (1959, 17). He criticised what he saw as the particularly English 'fanatical belief in educational specialisation, which is much more deeply ingrained in us than in any country in the world, west or east'. His solution was curriculum change:

> There is only one way out of all this: it is, of course, by rethinking our education.

The anthropologist Clifford Geertz (1982, 32) later observed the particularities of disciplinary cultures and the diverse ways in which we think in those disciplines. Like Snow, he argued that the modern world needs more interplay between disciplinary ways of thinking and being. Advocating better dialogue between people in different roles in higher education, he recognised that if there is to be genuine interplay between diverse disciplinary and professional positions, we must accept how deeply the differences in perspectives run and come to understand them better. We need also to 'construct some sort of vocabulary in which [these differences] can be publicly formulated', so that specialists in different areas can 'give a credible account of themselves to one another'.

New technologies have contributed to the building of more fluid academic networks; they have the capacity to spread emergent ideas and findings rapidly. The digitally connected, internationalised contexts in which disciplines act and develop are therefore even more fluid and permeable than they were at the start of this century. Reviewing curriculum in this context is timely: do our degree programmes reflect the shapes of emergent academic networks, ideas and findings?

Developments in interdisciplinary research

Addressing the possibilities afforded by connecting across disciplines in a research-based curriculum is particularly relevant at a time when research itself is moving in new interdisciplinary directions. A recent report by the British Academy (2016) highlights numerous contexts in which interdisciplinary research (IDR) is now taking place in the UK and beyond. It outlines challenges faced by researchers whose work cuts across established disciplines but also the benefits to knowledge production. The British Academy uses a broad working definition of IDR, which includes:

- Individual researchers' learning methods from other areas and applying them to issues that arise in their own discipline.
- Exploratory collaborations between disciplines to find areas of common interest – or to identify new approaches to issues within each respective discipline.
- Challenge- or question-focused research that requires the input of a range of disciplines working together – such as research in public health or sustainability.
- Emerging disciplines that bring together approaches from separate areas, for example biomedical engineering and digital humanities.
- Individuals or groups of researchers working in areas seen as inherently interdisciplinary because of the range of questions addressed or the range of approaches taken – such as Classics or Geography. (British Academy 2016, 8)

The British Academy study finds that the most frequently cited reasons given for interdisciplinary research is 'its essential role in addressing complex problems and research questions posed by global social challenges, as well as the increased rigour it can bring to one's understanding of one's own discipline' (2016, 9). It challenges here the assumption that to range across disciplines necessarily weakens the rigour in the 'home' discipline. A defence of traditional disciplines can always be made; see for example arguments put forward by Jacobs (2013), who defends the inherent richness and openness of established disciplines such as economics and biology. However, the focus of this dimension is not on dismantling distinctive disciplines but on building appropriate bridges between them in ways that strengthen them in a modern, digital world that increasingly connects across traditional knowledge boundaries.

5 Making a difference in the world

Revisiting our earlier emphasis on the potential of education to make an impact on 'the global common good', we consider the potential of engaging students in interdisciplinary and cross-disciplinary tasks that engage with and make a difference to the world. Situating subject-based learning in the wider context of both the students' overall development and contemporary global issues is not an aim readily accepted by all in academia. When Clifford (2009, 142) undertook research into the different attitudes among academics with respect to interdisciplinarity, for example, she found that some found it difficult to 'move away from a focus on "the science" to a focus on the holistic, personal and academic development of students'. She argues, however, that:

> Students need to grasp the concepts of theoretical science, but they will also be faced with using their science in the world, and they will need some understanding of global issues and [to] have ways of making ethical judgements about their work. Students will also need to be able to work within a multicultural environment wherever they are geographically located.

Connecting across disciplines does not speak only to intellectual connections and discoveries, then, but to global and ethical awareness. Recent work on school curriculum by Boix Mansilla and Chua (2016) at the Harvard Graduate School of Education is relevant here. Their focus on 'signature pedagogies' (see Shulman 2005) in global competence education highlights the value of preparing students, in terms of both skills and attitudes, for a complex and changing global landscape.

Boix Mansilla and Chua (2016, 3) define global competence as 'the capacity and disposition to understand and act on issues of global significance'. They characterise three key areas of focus:

- Firstly, global competence is cast as a capacity to understand – to use disciplinary concepts, theories, ideas, methods or findings in novel situations, to solve problems, produce explanations, create products or interpret phenomena in novel ways.

- Secondly, if 'understanding' speaks of depth and flexibility in subject matter expertise, 'global competence' as a disposition speaks of depth in terms of student ownership and transformation.
- Finally, as global competence focuses on issues of global significance and action to improve conditions, learning must be visibly relevant to students and the world. When significance is considered, global competence curricula becomes a call for authenticity, for carefully looking to the contemporary world for topics that matter most to examine.

These themes echo the orientation and values of the Connected Curriculum approach: building new knowledge and analyses, promoting student ownership and transformation, and making a difference to the world in ways that are relevant to diverse students. If there was ever a time when these are relevant it is now: the political upheavals in the United States and in Europe in 2016 have contributed to an extraordinary period of global change and challenge. Students are entitled to engage with global issues as they study and to develop knowledge and critical insights that can underpin their agency in the world.

This work by Boix Mansilla and Chua prompts us to consider again how we are currently engaging students with global themes and challenges in our curricula. Can curriculum design features such as 'Connections' modules, academic tutorials or a capstone module (Chapter 4) or outwards-facing assessments and/or a Showcase Portfolio (Chapter 7) be catalysts for enhanced student learning in this area? For example, one Connections module might address the idea of global issues directly, challenging students to work in groups on a given theme, while at the same time prompting students to make connections between the themes and topics they have learned elsewhere on the programme. The curated Showcase Portfolio approach could allow students to undertake an independent study on a global issue that is a topic of interest to them personally and include that in the Portfolio, together with a brief analytic commentary on what has been learned and on how the study has shed light on their wider learning.

There is no one 'right' approach for departments and programme teams. The aim here is to consider a range of possibilities for students to make connections across disciplines and link these ideas to global themes that might be enriched and extended.

6 Conclusions

Making connections across disciplines is not a territory whose pathways every academic and every student will walk easily. Von Humboldt argued that:

> there are naturally many who are active (in the university) to whom tendency towards depth and breadth is alien and there will be some to whom it is repugnant. … It need, however, find expression only occasionally, here and there, to have a widespread and enduring impact. (Cited in Morgan 2011, 332)

It remains vital for specialisms to sustain themselves as rich intellectual spaces. However, the wider world beckons for students just as it does for research with its multiple strands of enquiry. Providing gateways in the curriculum from one discipline to another for students has the potential to strengthen and deepen their critical and creative faculties as practised in the home discipline. Where it is possible to open up shared spaces for making enquiries about the world that draw on the content and practices of more than one discipline, students can develop the breadth and adaptability needed for a rapidly changing social, economic and international landscape. They can also see their home discipline(s) through more educated eyes.

Connecting the curriculum along this dimension forges both intellectual links across disciplines and opportunities for students to relate their learning and enquiry to the world around them. In the following chapter we look in more detail at how students can make explicit links between academic and workplace learning.

7 Vignettes of practice

The vignettes of practice here highlight some of the ways in which programmes of study are engaging students in cross-disciplinary and inter-disciplinary investigations. The first shows how chemists and physicists at UCL combine their knowledge to tackle a complex scenario. The second describes a cross-disciplinary undergraduate group research project at the London School of Economics and Political Science, and the third introduces a scheme whereby students work in multi-disciplinary teams in the UCL Faculty of Engineering to develop practical solutions to societal and environmental challenges.

1. Cross-disciplinary scenarios in an undergraduate Chemistry degree at UCL

Our research focuses on searching for new types of physical (magnetic) behaviour, often in materials that appear deceptively simple. Looking for the extraordinary and properties that we don't know enough about to even predict, calls on us to be able to recognise inconsistencies and identify what makes an observation remarkable. The research is not one of classification but of taxonomy based on deductive logic and the isolation of behaviours. The skills for this research are far more sophisticated than the skills of a standard undergraduate course – it cannot succeed without strong abilities to precisely translate ideas from simpler situations, to critique and logically to analyse situations, and to recognise when new classifications are needed. Experiments need to be invented and data scrutinised in the effort to reveal these extraordinary characteristics.

Undergraduates are challenged when asked to apply these skills within such an open-ended scenario. In part, this follows from our current degree programmes not allowing both physics and materials chemistry to develop as specialisations. Those that have done more physics typically have a weaker knowledge of chemistry concepts, such as atomic bonding, and less experience in synthesising materials. Those that have studied more materials chemistry will know less of the exotic quantum mechanical rules that underlie magnetic properties, and so are less familiar with the foundation concepts of the theoretical models. Having such clear deficits in their knowledge forces students to return to their foundation material and redevelop it quickly into this research context: ideas are liberated from the confinement of lecture courses. This is because the ideas cannot simply be translated, they have to be adapted and extended in response to a continuing programme of research. They are given depth and reality. In the experimental sciences this creative redefinition of knowledge is called for time and time again by the need to understand the results of experiments, to create logical deductions, to define the next research question and construct a suitable study. Eventually what was once learned becomes unlearned, recreated and assimilated into an understanding of the research field.

By the end of the final year research project the undergraduates have not only gained experience at a frontier of research, they have become scientists that are able to critically reconstruct the earlier lessons of their degree. They question. They no longer see the material of the course as static. It has become a fluid understanding that is allowed to evolve and grow.

Submitted by Dr Andrew Wills, Reader in the UCL Department of Chemistry, and a UCL Connected Curriculum Fellow.

2. Cross-disciplinary research groups in the social sciences at London School of Economics and Political Science (LSE), UK

LSE GROUPS is an intensive, undergraduate group research project, run by LSE Teaching and Learning Centre. It takes place in the last two weeks of the summer term each academic year. Students from across the School are placed in cross-year, cross-disciplinary groups and undertake an original research project under a broad overarching theme. Recent themes have included 'Social Change in London' and 'Poverty and Inequality in London'.

In the course of two weeks, students come up with a research question, review the relevant literature, choose an appropriate methodology, collect and analyse data, write up a research paper and present it at an academic conference on the final day. Each group is supported by a research supervisor, usually PhD students well advanced in their doctorates, and through resource sessions on different aspects of the research process.

LSE GROUPS is underpinned by an enquiry-based learning philosophy; the students learn about research and knowledge creation by undertaking research themselves. Meanwhile the supervisors are also melded in a community of practice through daily meetings and reflective discussions. For students and research supervisors alike, LSE GROUPS is a transformative educational experience. As one student commented: 'Our ideas became the focus of our investigation in LSE GROUPS, whereas they are only secondary in undergraduate courses. The supervisors guide you but you do the thinking for yourself, rather than being told what to think.'

Vignette of practice submitted by Dr Claire Gordon, Head of LSE Teaching and Learning Centre and Director of LSE GROUPS.

3. 'How to Change the World' in Engineering

UCL's 'How to Change the World' programme is a credit bearing, intensive, two-week programme involving over 700 students from

(Continued)

across the Engineering Faculty. Students work in multi-disciplinary teams of five to six developing practical solutions to societal and environmental challenges set by external organisations such as Arup, the Department for Transport and the International Committee of the Red Cross. The challenges resonate across sectors and are international in nature: for example, energy generation in rural African locations; reducing urban congestion; and increasing access to safe drinking water and sanitation.

The programme:

- enables students to see how their own discipline interacts with other disciplines;
- assists students in articulating their strengths;
- reflects business practice in the workplace – the challenges are intentionally loosely defined so that the students refine the brief in consultation with their challenge partner;
- takes groups of students through each stage of the design process from researching and clarifying the client's needs to meeting industry experts to working up a prototype and a design solution;
- provides all students with a client-facing consultancy style project, which they can market to employers;
- focuses on delivering tangible outputs – the students pitch their proposals to the challenge partners and academics at the end of the programme;
- encourages self-reflection: students produce an individual, self-reflective video relating to their experience;
- facilitates the development of the skills employers identify as lacking (e.g. commercial awareness, communication and team-working skills);
- provides opportunities to meet alumni and employers and explore career opportunities;
- reflects the techniques used by employers to assess candidates such as group exercises, presentations and self-reflection on performance.

Student teams are self-managed, with an innovative probation system managed by the students themselves to resolve any team-based issues. The programme leads up to 'Dragons' Den' style presentations with the proposed solutions being judged by industry partners and academics; and a Careers Expo involving employers from across the engineering sector.

The programme has been operating since 2014, with annual refinements based upon student and other partner feedback. Forty challenge partner organisations were involved in the 2016 programme together with UCL research staff and entrepreneurial and legal support (for teams wishing to develop their ideas further). The scale of the programme is such that it provides an opportunity for all second-year students in the Engineering Faculty.

Submitted by Mark De Freitas. In his role as Careers Consultant at UCL, Mark reviewed and promoted this programme, which was developed by Dr Kate Roach and UCL's Department of Science Technology, Engineering and Public Policy.

6

Connecting academic learning with workplace learning

1 Academic learning and work

The fourth dimension of the Connected Curriculum framework 'Students connect academic learning with workplace learning', shine a light upon a longstanding challenge for universities. The dimensio promotes the idea that all programmes of study should give students th chance to connect academic learning explicitly with the areas of know edge, skills and approaches needed both for professional work and fc their future lives in society. They should enable students to become life long learners. One focus here is on developing capabilities and persona attributes for life and work in a changing world. Political, economic an technological innovations are constantly shaping and changing wor related structures and processes. Another focus is on raising student levels of awareness that they *are* developing a rich range of unde standings, skills, values and attributes to take with them into their pr fessional lives, and on enabling them to practise articulating these others. The third area of focus is on enabling students to engage in cri ical and constructive dialogue with others about the ethical applicatic of evidence-based knowledge to society; this may include thinking cri ically about the nature and processes of work itself.

For many, it is self-evident that higher education 'involves pr paring students in ways that will equip them to engage successful with the world beyond university' (Spencer, Riddle and Knewstul 2012, 217). However, a recent study published by the Higher Educatic Academy (2016), analysing results of the UK Engagement Surve (Neves 2016), suggests that students are not yet convinced that the academic studies are preparing them well for work. This large-sca survey of undergraduates, developed under licence from the National Survey of Student Engagement (NSSE) in the United States, sets out to measure students' engagement with their studies in relation to a number of themes. Findings show that although most students (88 per cent) say they find their programme challenging and that they engage in critical thinking by applying facts, theories and methods (83 per cent), many fewer report that they have interacted with staff to discuss academic performance (36 per cent) and talk about their career plans (20 per cent) (Neves 2016, 12). And while many students report engaging in critical thinking (77 per cent of students in universities established before 1992 and 79 per cent in Post-92 universities), only 55 per cent of students in Pre-92 institutions and 66 per cent in Post-92 institutions report having engaged in research and enquiry. These data suggest that many students do *not* see themselves as regularly participating in research and enquiry, developing 'civic skills' or making preparations for their careers. Neves concludes from the data overall that 'there are clear opportunities for students to engage more regularly with staff, and their peers, in order to ensure development of a full range of career and civic skills', and that 'Career skills in particular are potentially an area for greater investigation and action across the sector, building on the low levels of development reported here' (Neves 2016, 34).

Interestingly, Neves' analysis suggests that students who collaborate most with their peers and with staff are also the most likely to report positively on their career skill development, and that there is work for institutions to do in these areas; these are areas addressed across the Connected Curriculum framework, particularly as we turn the spotlight on the fourth dimension.

2 The challenge of 'employability'

The UK Commission for Employment and Skills (2010) has argued that universities should pay more attention to developing both curricula and teaching staff in order to improve students' work-related attributes:

> The prize for securing real improvements in the delivery of employability skills is that we develop more individuals with the skills necessary to get a job that is fulfilling and offers a real platform for progression in work.

In the UK, the term 'employability' is often used but it has slippery definitions as Blackmore et al. (2016) demonstrate. Typically, it refers to:

> the development of a 'combination' or 'set of achievements' of skills, knowledge, understanding, and personal attributes that together make a graduate more likely to gain and remain in employment. (Blackmore et al. 2016, 10)

However, the term is also used more broadly, to include the development of skills and dispositions for living:

> Within this wider definition, employability is also considered in terms of its societal contribution and benefit to a range of stakeholders beyond the student, such as the workforce, community, and economy. (Blackmore et al. 2016, 10)

Emphasis in the literature is thus not only on students' readiness for work – that is, on their being prepared for particular, existing roles – but on developing a range of skills, capabilities and attributes, in tandem with discipline-specific knowledge and skills, which will enable students to 'manage their own careers and … continue learning throughout their working lives' (Mason, Williams and Cranmer 2009, 2).

There have been a number of studies looking at ways of characterising graduate attributes, which overlap of course with discipline-specific learning outcomes, and these can be framed in various ways. Knight and Yorke (2006a) cite, for example, a characterisation of four influential components:

- understanding
- skills (or skilful practices)
- students' efficacy beliefs and self-theories
- metacognition; that is, students' self-awareness in relation to learning and 'the capacity to reflect on, in and for action'.

(Knight and Yorke 2006a, 5)

Rees, Forbes and Kubler (2007) devise, building on the UK Quality Assurance Agency's subject benchmark statements for honours degree subjects (QAA 2016a), a set of profiles for different disciplines, which draw collectively on a broad list of capabilities. These include a wide range of attributes varying from achievement orientation, commercial awareness and image, to analysis, creativity and listening (2007, 141–142).

A number of institutions in the UK have developed their own sets of 'graduate attributes', including the University of Glasgow (2016), University of Edinburgh (2016) and University of Sheffield (2016). The University of Edinburgh, for example, distils its attributes into what its graduates are expected to have, and what they are expected to be.

Graduates have:

- curiosity for learning that makes a positive difference;
- courage to expand and fulfil their potential;
- passion to engage locally and globally.

Graduates are:

- creative problem solvers and researchers;
- critical and reflective thinkers;
- effective and influential contributors;
- skilled communicators.

These broad-brush characterisations of dispositions and skills can stimulate thinking about curriculum development and also about the importance of exploring with students the kinds of attributes they are already developing as they study their chosen discipline(s).

However, it is at programme and module level that these attributes are developed. What options are available to programme leaders and teams? We look next at how programme design can be maximised to empower students to prepare for their future working lives.

3 Practical approaches for curriculum design

If we are to take up the challenge of maximising students' opportunities to take ownership of their futures, we need to consider the ways in which programmes can be designed to do this. A number of publications offer useful advice for institutions on how to review curricula to embed skills for employment (see, for example, Cole and Tibby 2013; Knight and Yorke 2006a and 2006b; Smith 2012). The UK Higher Education Academy (2016) has also produced a set of studies highlighting principles for embedding employability into curricula.

However, a number of the design features and pedagogies inherent in the Connected Curriculum framework already lend themselves to enhancing students' opportunities for developing work-related attributes. We revisit those briefly here, and look at additional ways in which learning opportunities can be built into the curriculum that will enable students to graduate with confidence.

Our emphasis so far has been upon research-based and enquiry-based pedagogies and also on addressing the structure of taught programmes to create (or enhance) a connected throughline of activity that allows students to develop over time. We have begun to look, too, at the role played by student assessments in shaping their learning experiences and in enabling them to express their new learning to others (see further, Chapter 7). These features all engage students actively in the development of a wide range of transferable skills as an intrinsic part of their learning and assessment activities.

Tynjälä, Välimaa and Sarja (2003) find that institutions are already narrowing the gap between the kinds of learning students experience in their studies and that experienced in the workplace. Learning in the workplace is typically less formal, more collaborative and more specifically situated in a given 'real world' context, whereas academic learning has traditionally focused on broad principles. However, 'pedagogical models such as problem-based learning, project learning and collaborative learning have characteristics that simulate authentic situations in working life or may be even based on them' (2003, 152).

What different ways are there of enabling students to make explicit and productive connections between their academic learning and workplace learning during their programmes of study? They are many and varied, and institutions and departments are best equipped to make their own choices about what will be effective within the context of particular programmes.

Blackmore et al. (2016, 20) distinguish between 'bolt-on studies', defined as 'activities that sit outside of specific academic modules, but still relate to the curriculum', and activities embedded into the curriculum itself. Bolt-on studies include 'extra-curricular opportunities, workshops, or optional courses [which are] not a part of the essential credit-bearing modules in a degree programme'. Optional opportunities beyond the curriculum have the benefit of giving a wider range of choices and freedoms than a planned curriculum can typically manage. They may have challenges, though, with respect to equality of opportunity: students whose 'spare' time is taken up with duties such as caring or paid work are less likely to be able to benefit from them.

Embedding work-related learning activities in the curriculum, and enabling students to analyse and articulate these, can take a wide range of forms. Some are illustrated in Table 6.1. This is by no means an exhaustive list, but the range is indicative of the many and varied ways

Table 6.1 Activities connecting students with workplace learning

	Learning activity	Opportunities and Challenges
1	**Learning the knowledge content and skills inherent in the home discipline(s)**	Students' development of discipline-specific knowledge and skills is the central focus of any programme. Depth in subject-specific knowledge and understanding can be enhanced by illustrating these with reference to work-related challenges but this is dependent upon forging authentic links. For subjects not directly linked with particular professions, inviting alumni to discuss with students how the subject content and skills have helped them in diverse work-related contexts can be helpful.
2	**Learning through signature tasks and assessments in the home discipline(s)**	Each discipline has its typical assessment methods, both informal and formal, and many departments now include 'authentic' assessments (Knight 2002), which mirror the types of tasks needed in the workplace. A well designed spectrum of tasks enables students to develop skills such as teamwork, digital literacies and project management. These 'soft' skills can be assessed alongside subject-specific knowledge and skills, using appropriate assessment criteria with agreed weightings. For example, a group oral presentation can include criteria for content (e.g. critical analysis) and also for form (e.g. the structure and delivery of the presentation; the use of digital media). Randomly challenging students with different types of task, without the opportunity to build up skills and confidence, is unhelpful. However, well planned variations in tasks and assessments which build on one another will stretch and engage students.
3	**Learning through engaging in active enquiry**	Learning through active enquiry includes research, problem-solving, collaborative projects and object-based learning. These complex assignments, both collaborative and independent, can mirror closely workplace activities. Students need regular guidance, with dialogue, so that they can get the most from these more open-ended tasks. The guidance can include prompts to help students appreciate the range of skills they are developing.

(Continued)

Table 6.1 (Continued)

	Learning activity	Opportunities and Challenges
4	Learning through engaging in enterprise and/or entrepreneurship	Broadly defined, enterprise education 'provides individuals with the skills, tools and insights to enable them to create ideas and make them happen' (Blackmore et al. 2016, 28). Entrepreneurship is defined as 'the application of enterprise skills specifically to creating and growing organisations in order to identify and build on opportunities' (QAA 2012). Students can be stretched, within or beyond the taught curriculum, by engaging in broadly based, creative, typically collaborative tasks in which they have to show initiative and resourcefulness. Entrepreneurial activities are usually but not always undertaken alongside the taught curriculum. Students can be explicitly prompted to see the connections between these experiences and those needed for the workplace.
5	Learning through making, creating and/or performing	Making new objects (in any subject), producing works of art and putting on performances all develop a broad range of skills and dispositions, such as time management and leadership, along with creativity. Such activities give students something unique to show future employers. Students may need to be prompted, however, to be able to articulate clearly the skills and personal qualities their productions have demonstrated, and their relevance to challenges in other contexts.
6	Learning by engaging with broad societal themes	Students explore a crosscutting theme, for example sustainability (QAA 2014), either within a programme, across programmes (for example, via a cross-disciplinary module), or via extra-curricular opportunities. Following a societal theme throughout their studies can give students confidence in looking at that field from a range of perspectives, as well as considering the values that they can take into the workplace.
7	Learning *about* the workplace and future employment opportunities	Students set out to find out about workplace opportunities. Careers centres and alumni can help here, as faculty members may not be best placed to advise students in the rapidly changing world of work. In some programmes, it might be appropriate for students to investigate an aspect of working life and/or a specific profession, and/or engage in work shadowing, as part of the formal curriculum.
8	Learning through study and/or work abroad	Students benefit greatly from studying and/or working abroad (European Union 2014). Studying abroad and learning additional languages are among the most effective ways of developing skills and experiences that can be demonstrated to future employers. Skills developed, including interpersonal skills, resilience and openness

9	**Learning through volunteering and other extra-curricular activities**	Students participate in activities ranging from following personal interests (e.g. in music or sport) to engaging in wider opportunities provided by the institution (e.g. working as a student intern; becoming a student representative; participating in university-wide events and talks; participating in Student Union activities). The range of opportunities is so wide, and students' engagement with them so variable, that it is not easy to capture the benefits they are making to students in helping to prepare them for work. Reflective analyses of these wider experiences can, however, be explored in a personal or professional log or blog, and even in an assessed programme-wide portfolio (Chapter 7).
10	**Learning through becoming a leader and 'agent for change' in their institution**	Institutions invite students to run 'change projects', with the aim of benefiting current and future student cohorts (Healey 2016; UCL 2016h). Run at institutional and/or departmental level, such schemes can be mutually beneficial for students and the institution. Students can be invited to conceptualise, design, lead on (or participate in) and be rewarded for change projects. This entails managing a funded project, managing resources and time, and presenting project outcomes to an audience. Experience of this kind is excellent for students' future employment prospects, as well as connecting students with departmental and institutional communities.
11	**Service-learning**	Students participate in a community-based project or activity, typically in collaboration with other students, for example by contributing to the work of a local charity. Direct engagement with the community for mutual benefit, as part of the overall aims and ethos of a programme of study, can provide excellent learning experiences as well as activities which are meaningful in their own right. Reflective analysis of the project and the student's role in it can form part of their summative assessment. Room needs to be given in the assessment criteria for learning from mistakes and difficulties, as well as from obvious successes.
12	**Work-based learning**	Students undertake a programme which is orientated towards a specific profession and/or workplace setting, and which has been designed from the outset to embed work-based learning throughout the programme, for example with mandatory work placements (Boud and Solomon 2001). These experiences are typically assessed through students' analyses of their own work via a professional log and/or credit-bearing assignment. The extent to which students are prepared for this experience, and are helped to bring their academic learning into their workplace challenges, varies; they can benefit from discussing some of these connections before the placement starts.

in which students are already developing their work-related knowledge and skills, and of where they might have additional opportunities extended to them.

The ways in which departments and programme leaders select from – and add to – these options will depend on many contextual factors. Useful practices for most programmes, however, include:

1. **Designing some student learning activities that mirror the 'messy' ways in which learning takes place in the workplace.** Asking students to address challenges as they arise during their studies by using their own initiative to investigate solutions, by tracking down and tapping into relevant expertise (whether in-house or external) and by collaborating effectively with their peers are examples of activities that will prepare them for the typically unstructured learning demands of the workplace.

2. **Requiring students explicitly to analyse and articulate their learning**, both in core disciplinary areas and more widely, and its relevance to the workplace at intervals through their study. Attention needs to be paid to how and when students will be asked explicitly to analyse and articulate their developing skills, values and attributes. Developing these attributes unknowingly does not help students to articulate connections they have made between academic and work-related learning (Knight and Yorke 2006b), and this is an important aspect of this dimension of the Connected Curriculum framework.

3. **Building in a core portfolio and/or summative task**, for example through a series of Connections modules and/or a capstone module (see Chapter 3), in which students describe clearly the skills and attributes they have developed, in ways which are meaningful to the student personally and authentically linked to subject knowledge.

4. **Ensuring that some assessments are addressed to diverse audiences** and so develop a wide range of digital and communication skills. This theme will be addressed further in the next chapter.

4 Critiquing the connection between academic learning and workplace learning

While many scholars have been supportive of closer connections between academic and work-related learning, others have raised doubts about the growing attention given to 'employability'. They critique some of the underpinning assumptions associated with this emphasis, questioning the employment focus both in terms of its alleged benefits to students as individuals and the potential impact on society more widely.

One critique relates to the idea that academia should be a creative space in which scholars, both faculty members and students, can explore knowledge and understandings that may have no obvious relationship with the workplace. Sometimes encapsulated in the phrase 'knowledge for knowledge's sake', this position sees knowledge as intrinsically improving our quality of life. It alludes to the personal fulfilment associated with following one's own interests and building up one's ability to learn, without any immediate instrumental purpose. This notion was dismissed as elitist 'piffle' by Ferdinand von Prondzynsk, Principal of Robert Gordon University, in a recent THE article (THE 2013). However, there are echoes here of the cherished 'Haldane principle' in research, which holds that governments should not, via any funding arrangement, be able to 'exert undue influence' on the research undertaken (Boden and Nedeva 2010, 39). Does academic freedom, including the freedom to explore non-commercial, non-applied areas of knowledge, become threatened by calls to ensure that students are learning work-related knowledge and skills?

Further tensions in academia have arisen, in the UK at least, with respect to the relationship between funding and 'employability metrics'. The latter are built into the government's Teaching Excellence Framework (QAA 2016b), in which levels of graduate employment are included in the criteria for institutional assessment. Imperatives relating to employment and contributing to a successful economy are thus caught up in academic critiques of forms of 'new managerialism' (Deem, Hillyard and Reed 2007), which find their expression in quality management regimes and audit cultures (Apple 2005; Morley 2003).

There is even a sense for some scholars that:

> employability discourses may be adversely affecting pedagogies and curricula, to the disbenefit of students, institutions, employers, social justice and civil society. (Boden and Nedeva 2010, 37)

Boden and Nedeva argue that, where in the past universities have regarded graduate employment as an aspect of institutions' relationships with the labour market in which they have 'enjoyed a significant degree of discretion', employability is now 'a performative function of universities, shaped and directed by the state, which is seeking to supplant labour markets'. Their analysis reminds us that what is at stake as we address academic learning-workplace connections is the role of universities today:

> the issue of the relationship between higher education and working life is ... the question structuring the relationship between higher education and society. (Tynjälä, Välimaa and Sarja 2003, 149)

Revisiting the principles of the Connected Curriculum initiative may, for some, help to resolve tensions between academic freedoms and preparing students for the world of work. While it may be possible to hold and promote a conception of education as developing both individuals and societies through active, critical enquiry, whereby knowledge is extended and refined through peer dialogue for the global common good, it is not obvious that there are any *necessary* tensions between academia and developing students' opportunities for employment. Need there be a conflict between developing oneself in the round as a critical, curious, creative, engaged individual and developing one's ability to work successfully in society and contribute to the good of society more broadly? Where 'employability' becomes reified, for example in any imposition of fixed lists of attributes for assessment or in narrowly conceived pedagogic imperatives, or where it becomes tied up with political imperatives, clearly there are potential issues for disciplines and their practices, and scholars will rightly engage critically with these issues. However, developing self-aware students through enabling them to engage regularly in active, critical research and enquiry has the potential to *empower* them not only to develop their own capabilities and values but also to critique society, including the role played by work in local and global communities.

In many institutions, academics continue to exercise significant amounts of freedom to interpret challenges to 'connect with the workplace' in ways which complement their disciplinary cultures and departmental values. Institutional initiatives may prompt programme teams to review their curriculum design in the light of workplace-related themes, but few dictate specific requirements in this area. The latter approach could be very counter-productive; requiring academics, who have developed high-level critical thinking skills, to work with an imposed set of fixed requirements would be a risky strategy.

The Connected Curriculum framework assumes that there *need* be no contradiction between developing students intellectually as critical citizens and preparing them for the workplace. In the spirit of forwarding shared understandings through the meetings of different knowledge horizons, collaborating with employers' groups and other relevant stakeholders can be very productive. Connected Curriculum principles also assume that research-based curriculum design can develop intellectual enquiry and practical, applied knowledge simultaneously, particularly if the programme, even if modular in construction, is designed as a coherent whole (Chapter 4).

5 Vignettes of practice

The first illustrative vignette in this chapter comprises two accounts, written by students on the interdisciplinary UCL Bachelor of Arts and Sciences (BASc) programme, of their experiences of taking up summer internships. The second describes a non-assessed compulsory course for all taught masters students at the European Institute, LSE, and the third outlines ways in which internationally recruited students at the UCL Institute of Education are empowered to become effective and reflective teacher-researchers. The fourth describes how Masters students at the University of Sheffield benefited from volunteering to support excluded and isolated people, and the final vignette describes work-shadowing and observations at the UCL Institute of Neurology. Activities such as these, which are currently set up as being extra-curricular could also, in principle, form part of the assessed curriculum.

1. Internships on a Bachelor of Arts and Sciences (BASc) degree

As an integral part of UCL's interdisciplinary BASc programme, students undertake summer internships. Two students reflect here on their experiences.

Hugo Stevens
Over the summer, I joined PwC Legal's business development team in Paris for a ten-week internship. For the application process, I produced a CV with a covering letter and had an interview with a manager and a member of the HR team. I chose this internship because I thought it would enable me to test my interests in Law and Business management. I knew the firm was implementing a transformation programme and I was interested to see how it envisioned its future workplace. I ended up contributing to the development of the firm's Knowledge Management platform and having end-to-end responsibility for the creation of a firm-wide online storage and collaboration database.

(Continued)

I feel like the BASc had prepared me really well for this internship. My modules at UCL provided me with a wide-ranging understanding of how societies function and evolve. By studying managerial accounting for decision-making, I had learned how businesses are structured and managed, which was particularly relevant to my role. But the skills I learned through the BASc were truly the key to my success. First and foremost, my interdisciplinary education had taught me to approach complex problems from different perspectives. This polyvalence proved decisive, since I arrived at PwC without any prior knowledge of Customer Relationship Management and online database design. The ability to work in a team, a skill I had honed through repeated practice on my degree programme, was also crucial in a professional environment where relationships are becoming more and more horizontal. Finally, the computing skills I acquired through the Quantitative Methods core modules were put to good use, as PwC's work is technology-driven.

Irene Di Giorgio

I spent a month as an intern in a travel start-up based in Montecarlo. My positive experience there must be largely credited to the transferable skills gained during my time on the BASc programme. The three characteristics that I could identify both in the programme and my work experience are: team-working in an international professional environment, flexibility regarding ever-shifting tasks and creative problem solving.

A start-up tends to operate in a diametrically opposite fashion to a corporate environment in terms of hierarchy and problem-targeting. The blurring between job titles and the small size of the team means that any employee, even if highly specialised, will work very closely with colleagues with different kinds of expertise and varied backgrounds. Employees are also likely to participate at some stage in tasks dramatically out of their own field of knowledge.

The collaboration between different professional figures was paramount for resolving the ever-shifting and 'messy' interdisciplinary problems revolving around the product (the website). These challenges did not fall squarely into neat categories of, for instance, marketing, platform building, or creation of content. Having no set mode of working, the company acts on the creative insights of its team. This means that flexibility, adaptability and lateral thinking are indispensable skills in the workplace. My background in interdisciplinary research methods and Psychology helped me a great deal in the marketing tasks, allowing me autonomously to design customer questionnaires and interviews, while the grounding in the quantitative methods and coding made me integrate much more quickly with my main collaborators, the web developers.

Vignette submitted by Carl Gombrich, Director of the UCL BASc programme.

2. Engaging with Europe: Professional Skills at London School of Economics and Political Science (LSE), UK

'Engaging with Europe: Professional Skills' is a non-assessed compulsory course for all taught masters students at the European Institute, LSE. The programme embeds professional skills training workshops in the context of a high-profile professional speaker series.

Both lecture and workshop segments are purposefully grounded within European institutions, public policies and contemporary political debates. As a result, the professional skills content clearly maps onto the academic content of the degrees. Guest speakers, wherever possible programme alumni, introduce a specific professional skill (e.g., blog writing, speech writing, legislative drafting), contextualising it within a relevant 'European' institutional setting (for example, Parliament or Commission) or issue area (for example, monetary union or freedom of movement).

The following week, students attend a workshop on that same skill. Workshops use a variety of learning activities including individual work (such as interviewing), group work (such as speech writing and blogging) as well as simulation exercises (such as lobbying and legislative drafting). Students receive feedback on the professional outputs that they produce.

All final (revised) outputs are uploaded onto an electronic portfolio system that students can share with prospective employers. The course receives positive feedback from students who value its unique approach to subject-relevant professional skills development.

Vignette submitted by Dr Jennifer Jackson-Preece, Deputy Head of the European Institute & Associate Professor of Nationalism, LSE, course convenor and instructor.

3. Preparing internationally recruited students to become effective and reflective teacher-researchers at the UCL Institute of Education

The UCL Institute of Education and the Institute of Ismaili Studies jointly deliver a Secondary Teacher Education Programme (STEP)

(*Continued*)

that prepares internationally recruited students to become effective and reflective teacher-researchers. The programme philosophy is to enable students to understand the value of research as a way of improving teaching practice in their specific contexts and pursuing their personal continuous professional development. In this way they link their academic learning with future workplace learning.

Over two years students learn to engage critically with research and to consider the relevance of research for practising teachers in general and also for themselves in their specific home countries. Using core readings as a starting point, students are challenged to review their preconceptions relating to research and think more strategically about how they can make changes and improvements to existing practices. This theoretical understanding leads into the formulation of a proposal for research. On their research modules on the Master of Teaching and the MA Education (Muslim Societies and Civilisations), students learn about qualitative and quantitative research as well as about methodologies and methods that are specifically suitable for small-scale investigations within education. Students then carry out their proposed research within their teaching practice and produce a report or dissertation. The preferred frameworks are action research projects or case studies, and the research questions are always relevant to their specific teaching environments in their home countries. For example, one student used action research to investigate the relevance of music within Muslim Societies and Civilisations lessons in Canada, while another explored the concepts of diversity and pluralism within Muslim Societies and Civilisations lessons in India. Both of these students acknowledged the contextualised nature of their findings but made clear recommendations for teaching practice – changes which they have actively implemented and are still using.

Students are able to highlight their personal learning in relation to their theoretical and practical understanding of research, and to consider undertaking similar projects for their own developmental purposes in the future.

Vignette submitted by Nicole Brown, Lecturer in Education and STEP Programme Leader at the UCL Institute of Education.

4. Masters students volunteering to support excluded and isolated people at the University of Sheffield, UK

In October 2014 a group of Masters students from the Information School at the University of Sheffield were recruited as volunteers for SAVTE (the Sheffield Association for the Voluntary Teaching of

English), supporting some of Sheffield's most excluded and isolated people via our local public library networks and the national Six Book Challenge (now Reading Ahead). The students supported English language or conversation classes in one of four venues in Sheffield, including a women's refuge, a primary care centre, a community room within a block of flats, and a conversation club.

For the students, participation makes a valuable addition to their CV, via a volunteering role with a third-sector organisation. Curricular impact and outputs include reflective pieces for an online professional development journal, coursework and dissertation options relating to the students' experience and the role of public libraries in adult literacy education. In terms of extra-curricular impact the project has helped the volunteers to develop skills in cultural awareness and civic engagement.

For the academic department, this has been an effective way of engaging with the local community, in particular with some of the most vulnerable people living in Sheffield. Now in the third academic year of the project, we are continuing to recruit volunteers and to link elements of our curriculum to the workplace, adding value to the Masters programmes.

The students are engaged and enthusiastic throughout the project and there has been a noticeable (and reported) increase in awareness of the application of academic learning to the community, as the following comments illustrate:

'The experience has given me a greater appreciation of the variety of needs and challenges facing members of my community. This will be beneficial in future jobs within libraries as I will now be more aware of attempting to ensure their needs are met and they feel welcome and valued.'

'I would certainly recommend participating in this project, as it provides you with a wonderful opportunity to support and help others…it is an incredibly rewarding experience.'

Case submitted by Dr Briony Birdi, Senior Lecturer in the Information School at the University of Sheffield. This project was initially funded by the University's Engaged Curriculum initiative, which aims to work with the local community in mutually beneficial ways.

5. Work-shadowing and observations lead to oral presentations and contributions to a patient newsletter at UCL Institute of Neurology

Students on the Stroke MSc programme are invited to undertake clinical observership placements on the Hyperacute Stroke Unit.

(Continued)

They are introduced to the opportunities during a lecture series on the clinical manifestations and hyperacute treatment of stroke. Observing practice enables them to see how evidence-based stroke treatment is being implemented in a clinical environment. They then participate in a session in which they consider their own place within that context and also how this links with both the London and world-wide systems for the treatment of stroke. We consider their future professional identity, how they would feel working in that environment and what specific professional challenges they might face.

Students also shadow the stroke research team in order to understand how patients are recruited to large multicentre trials. They observe the challenges faced when doing this and develop their understandings of the structure of the stroke research network. They address themes that are key in the clinical system, such as 'door to needle' times for treatment and optimisation of delivery of thrombolytic agents.

Giving oral presentations on the underpinning evidence, current situation and possibilities for further research within the theme of their choice, students are also given the opportunity to write for a stroke newsletter for patients, with distribution throughout South London. They explain what they think would be the most high-impact development in stroke treatment over the coming years, and why. This allows them to connect the academic material with the patient cohort that they would be working with as researchers in the future and to learn skills that would enable them to communicate complex ideas effectively.

Submitted by Dr Sumanjit Gill, Professor David Werring and Dr Robert Simister of the UCL Institute of Neurology.

Outward-facing student assessments

Revisiting student assessments

Dimension five of the Connected Curriculum framework focuses on assessing students' learning, and on the value for students of learning to produce 'outputs' – assessments directed at an audience. As they develop their learning through enquiry, students can become increasingly aware of people and groups in wider society who may have an interest or stake in those areas of learning. Through some of the work they produce for the purpose of being assessed by faculty members, they can engage with internal and/or external audiences. Some student assessments become, in effect, outputs from their research and enquiry. In expressing their new learning in different forms and language registers to different audiences, students enhance their communication skills and digital practices. Where possible, students' work will make an impact on local and wider audiences, and enable not only information-sharing but two-way engagement between students and audience.

Why is this emphasis important? Assessing students' learning in higher education is a high-stakes activity. As well as being extremely time-consuming, both for students and for assessors, assessment can determine students' futures. By designing particular kinds of student assignments, educators are shaping the ways in which students orientate themselves to their studies. By ascribing grades or scores that translate to a particular degree classification, assessors may be significantly affecting students' opportunities for further study or access to a profession. And by providing feedback on assessment tasks, assessors are not only giving information about progress and attainment but affecting students' self-confidence and self-concept.

The range of forms of student assessment used across the sector is growing (Bryan and Clegg 2006), and Knight (2002) argues that we need to make students' experiences of assessment as authentic, effective and efficient as possible. How can we do this – for students, for teachers and assessors, and even for wider society?

2 Towards authentic assessment

What is the traditional student assessment cycle? Table 7.1 offers a broad-brush summary.

After this cycle is complete, or even before completion, the cycle may begin again with attention directed towards another assessment. In modular or multi-stranded programmes, assessment cycles may run simultaneously, challenging students to juggle with multiple deadlines.

Table 7.1   Traditional student assessment cycle

	Traditional sequence of activities in student assessment cycle
1	Students take a class and/or undertake independent learning (e.g. via a virtual learning environment, through wider reading or experiential learning).
2	Students are informed about the assessment, or sequence of assessments, for this learning theme/phase.
3	Students are informed (to varying degrees) about the criteria that will be used to allocate marks or grades for that assessment.
4	Students are given instructions and advice about how to approach the assessment.
5	Students may undertake developmental, formative assessment to gain some feedback on their progress in this area of learning, before submitting their formally assessed (that is, summative) work.
6	Students prepare for their summative assessment, either individually or in collaboration with peers (where the latter is permitted and required).
7	Students undertake the assessment (e.g. write the essay; complete the group project; give the presentation; sit the exam).
8	Students submit the assessment to the assessors, who are already experts in the field.
9	Students await feedback on the assessment, or at least for notification of agreed marks.
10	Feedback and/or marks are made available.
11	Students may or may not access the feedback on their work.
12	Students may or may not assimilate the feedback and actively use it to inform future approaches to learning and assessment.

Of course certain types of provision may differ from this considerably; for example, some online courses build assessments directly into online learning activities. The number, size and type of assessments can also vary greatly between subjects, as can the kinds of feedback and the length of time students wait for that feedback. However, the assessment cycle often follows this kind of pattern.

What changes if we look differently at some of these assessments and re-frame them as outward-facing outputs of enquiry? First, it is important to note that, if changes are made, the fundamental principles of good practice for assessment and feedback still apply. A number of scholars offer research-informed guidelines on these practices: see, for example, Bloxham and Boyd 2007; Nicol and Macfarlane-Dick 2006; Boud and Falchikov 2007; Evans 2013; and Clarke and Boud 2016. These studies make recommendations about issues such as the importance of aligning assessments to the learning activities and intended learning, the degrees of validity and reliability built into the design of the assessment method, and the fairness of marking. Also important are the timeliness and relevance of feedback to help students learn and the need to ensure that assessments are designed for and accessible by students with diverse backgrounds, experiences and accessibility needs (Wray 2013).

However, through a more research-based, connective curriculum we have the opportunity to imagine new possibilities for assessing students: by setting up some assessed activities to mirror the kinds of communications, including public engagement activities, that are undertaken by researchers and enquiring professionals in many fields. If outward-facing assessment opportunities are built thoughtfully into the overall pattern of assessments in the programme, for example by placing them at regular intervals in a connected 'throughline' of core activities (Chapter 4), they can also enable students to develop a unique personal learning story. This brings together two aspects of authenticity: assessments are experienced as genuine because students face 'real world' enquiry-based challenges *and* because students are able to express themselves in their own voices, through communication styles they (in groups and/or individually) have chosen.

3 Possibilities for practice

How might this work in practice? As is always the case with any learning design decision, there will be different possibilities and emphases in different disciplines, but four key questions need to be addressed:

- What kinds of 'outputs' might students produce?
- To whom is their research directed?
- How will students' research outputs be collated and curated?
- How will assessment and feedback processes be affected?

Each of these will be addressed in turn.

Outputs

In our digital world, which has expanded hugely the number of ways in which we can communicate with others, there are now numerous possibilities for assessment. Substituting just a selection of the traditional forms of assessment, such as timed examinations, essays, laboratory reports and short-answer tests, with outward-facing assessments opens up new possibilities for challenging and engaging students. Assessments in the form of outputs or products might include, for example:

- Narrated slide presentations (online)
- Web pages
- Blogs
- Podcasts
- Wikis
- Short videos, combined with analytical webpage commentary
- Film documentaries
- Poster displays (in real time and/or online)
- Exhibitions (for example, of designed products or artworks, or of the questions, tools and findings of research and enquiry)
- Simulation exercises, demonstrated to an audience
- Individual or group oral presentations, directed at a designated audience
- Multi-media presentations
- Demonstrations
- Performances
- Student-run events, such as an undergraduate research conference or an event for alumni or employers, where assessment of group work and/or event management may be included in the assessment criteria.

These are just some initial suggestions: different subject disciplines naturally orientate towards some but not others and, indeed, some of these assessment methods are already standard practice in certain fields. Disciplines will also add a number of different options that fit better with their disciplinary framing and culture. But even the brief range here indicates how many modes of communication may come into play if we look again at the possibility of enriching the traditional assessment range.

Some disciplines, for example Literary Studies and Philosophy, have the academic essay form very deeply embedded in disciplinary thinking and practice. Essays are sometimes heavily criticised for being anachronistic and difficult to assess reliably but there are good reasons for the longstanding love of the form. Developing an argument that is supported by evidence is of central importance and the aesthetic of the essay comes into play. The use of language in an essay takes on an aesthetic quality that raises it far above a pragmatic expression of knowledge, and is central to thinking, expertise and practice in a number of disciplines. So for some subjects the essay may still remain a dominant form. However, the essay form can be enriched if students are (sometimes) asked to consider a specific context and audience for a given essay; for example, to write as if it were to be published in a particular journal or read by a nominated readership such as a particular interest group. And of course essays can be supplemented by other forms of assessment, which stretch students in different ways.

Use of documentary film has huge potential for assessment, as yet untapped in many departments. The serious film documentary might even be seen as the modern equivalent of an essay. Russel Tarr (2016, 42) proposes that essay writing can be 'refreshed' by introducing students to the 'fine art form of documentary-making'. Having used it very effectively in a school setting when teaching history, he argues that this is a highly achievable activity for students, helping them to develop their research skills and powers of argument as well as media literacy, and even building confidence in using their voices when presenting to an audience.

The forms of assessment can be many. The key for this dimension of the Connected Curriculum approach is to see whether, at each level of study, some assessments can stretch students' digital and communication skills as they collaborate to create a product that will express their learning (knowledge, skills and attitudes) to nominated others.

Some educators may be daunted by the idea of asking students to use, and therefore develop, skills in areas with which they themselves are not familiar. This needs some thought: where will students get advice on how to develop those skills? But our underpinning premise of the value of learning through enquiry comes into play here. Many students in real life are likely to search online videos for advice on new skills, or elicit help from others via social networking. Others will have less digital and social capital, so providing some accessible guidance, perhaps with the help of university experts in digital education and resources, will be valuable. More experienced students can also help those who are less so, through peer or cross-phase mentoring (Chapter 8).

Audiences and partners

Who are the 'others' to whom students are directing their work? Again, there is a very wide spectrum of possibilities, from immediate peers to an unfamiliar audience on the other side of the world. They include:

- student peers in the same class;
- student peers taking a different class, in their own or a partner institution;
- student peers studying at a different level: for example, PhD students present their emerging research to final year undergraduates, or second years present to first years;
- school students (e.g. those studying the subject for an A Level examination or equivalent);
- students from an institution in a different country;
- a local organisation, such as a charity, residents' group or interest group;
- a national organisation, such as a professional body, employers' group or political party;
- a business, whether local, national or multi-national;
- practitioners in a given field;
- policy makers in a particular field;
- publishing companies;
- consumers of particular services (e.g. health or legal services);
- the general public, who have a personal interest in a particular topic (e.g. sustainability, dementia, street art, local history);
- alumni: graduates of their own programme of study and/or from the institution more widely.

Again, this list is just indicative – discipline specialists will select from it and use their own existing and potential contacts to add to it, including those with whom they already connect via their related research and/or professional activities.

Ideally, some assessments would not only be produced *for* an audience but developed in partnership with them. For example, students of statistics might engage with a local charity in order to undertake statistical analyses that will be of real benefit to it. Both the task and the product are then authentically orientated to the needs of the audience-partner. Where the audience comprises policy makers, then a department or programme leader might liaise with a policy maker in the design and content of the learning tasks themselves, in order to direct students' attention to the most current areas of focus.

Challenges for students include the need to be able to build up relevant skills and levels of confidence gradually; this means that whole programme design comes into play once again. It is important that if, in their second year of study students have to make a film documentary, they have had some low-stakes video-making practice in the previous year. The overall pattern of assessments through the programme needs to be mapped out and seen by both educators and students to form a coherent sequence of challenges. This mapping is very much easier if there is a connected 'throughline' of mandatory activities, for example through a sequence of mandatory or 'Connections' modules (Chapter 3).

Challenges for educators include the need to keep their own skills up-to-date; professional development in some areas may be helpful and, of course, there are resource implications for this. However, once in place, embedding this wider spectrum of assessment activities will also contribute to the ongoing development of relevant skills, as staff and students develop their approaches together via shared assessment and feedback experiences.

It may not always be easy to identify appropriate audiences, whether conceptual or 'real life'. Both are valuable but some experience with real-life audiences for all students, at some stage in their programme, raises the quality of experience. Care has to be taken not to exploit audiences for the students' benefits or to derail the intended learning. But the more the audience-focused task can be created collaboratively between the department, students and audience, the better.

The major challenge for educators is time. Planning changes, especially those which take academics out of their comfort zone, takes time and institutions committed to more authentic, research-based assessments need to take account of this in workload models (see Chapter 10). However, time can also be saved in the assessment processes if a programme is designed to work towards a curated, programme-level portfolio, which can reduce time spent on initial moderation and internal marking processes (Bloxham 2009).

Collation and curation of outputs: the Showcase Portfolio

As suggested when we considered the value of creating a connected sequence of enquiry-based activities that run through the programme (Chapter 4), one approach to assessment that offers much potential is that of asking students to create a programme-wide, or programme-long, portfolio. This has many possible benefits. Nicol and Macfarlane-Dick (2006) argue that, while students have been given more responsibility for learning in some respects in recent years, there has been far greater reluctance to give them increased responsibility for assessment processes, even low-stakes formative processes. Yet, if students are to be prepared for learning throughout life, they must learn to regulate their own learning as they progress through higher education. A programme-long portfolio, which students can shape and edit through the length of the programme, offers them a chance to take ownership of their learning over a period of time, creating a space for 'slow scholarship' (Harland et al. 2015).

What do we mean by a 'portfolio' in this context? As Clarke and Boud (2016) note, there are many kinds of portfolio. These can range from personal scrapbooks of analysis and reflection, to a collation of separate assessments, to explicit mapping against a set of professional standards (for example in teacher education), to an overarching portfolio that collates and curates separate items of work produced. In the latter case, students can connect the elements of their work, or their 'outputs', across the programme with a succinct, overarching, analytical narrative.

My argument is that, while all of these portfolio options are useful, the curated summative portfolio that shows to the viewer the best of the students' work has great promise. We might call this a Showcase Portfolio. A broader, underpinning portfolio that includes reflections on the students' own development and/or constitutes an unedited collation of all their work is of course valuable as a working document; this enables students to manage their own learning, including making and learning from mistakes, without opening all of their activity up to scrutiny by others. But knowing that their work will need finally to be selected and curated, shaped into an engaging whole, for external scrutiny focuses students' attention on important areas. A Showcase Portfolio challenges students to:

- review their work, as they select and perhaps edit for presentation;
- revisit and learn from feedback on their work, including feedback from peers and external audiences/partners;
- develop a holistic, analytic picture of the ground covered on the programme, including insights gained through active research and enquiry;
- develop a stronger sense overall of the discipline(s) and themes studied and the ways in which they relate to one another;
- articulate explicitly the perspectives and skills underpinning the range of work presented.

New technologies make developing a Showcase Portfolio for each degree programme a realistic possibility:

> Increasingly, sophisticated electronic portfolio platforms support the adaptation of portfolio material to many purposes. The ease with which learning artefacts can be stored and retrieved allows students to keep, manipulate and selectively share their work, revealing it selectively for any desired purpose. (Clarke and Boud 2016, 2)

This portfolio becomes a curated collection of evidence, drawn from the wider range of work across the programme as a whole. A programme-wide portfolio showcases both 'learning skills such as reflection, self-assessment and feedback', and, where appropriate, 'evidence of professional competencies such as clinical judgement and professional requirements, at increasingly complex levels' (Clarke and Boud 2016, 3).

An overall holistic portfolio, which spans a whole programme or perhaps more feasibly just the connected, mandatory core of a programme, enables ongoing feedback to become an embedded element and so remain at the centre of students' attention. For the final Showcase Portfolio students can even be asked to respond to the feedback in a narrative analysing their achievements. The Showcase approach also enables peer assessment and dialogue, and engagement with external audiences, to be included as part of the mapping of activity and analysis of achievement. Students then select from all of the different elements, in line with criteria decided on by the department, to showcase their best work and present themselves as knowledgeable, skilful individuals.

We noted earlier that time is the biggest challenge in the whole process: how can shifting emphasis to a programme-wide Showcase Portfolio save time – or, at least, save enough to make the time spent on the Showcase possible? Sue Bloxham has drawn on evidence to argue, persuasively, that much of the time currently spent on second marking and moderation of smaller tasks throughout the programme can be saved by taking a more holistic approach to students' achievements. Bloxham (2009) demonstrates, in her analysis of current practice, that we waste resources in our well-meaning attempts to ensure fairness as we not only mark but second-mark and moderate. While agreed marking rubrics with specified assessment criteria help with the development of shared under-standings, assessment is not an exact science and can never be entirely objective. Rather than spending so much time on quality assurance pro-cesses in relation to the smaller tasks, the answer could be to accept a degree of subjectivity in the marking at that level and put more time into making quality judgements of the students' best work overall:

> The focus would shift from individual assessments to the overall profile of a student on the basis that a series of marks awarded over a period of time might provide a more accurate assessment of stu-dents. (Bloxham 2009, 216)

This suggests the possibility of a more focused role for external exam-iners, with emphasis placed on making a safe judgement on the basis of the programme-wide Showcase Portfolio.

This approach to assessment could mean re-thinking some of the practices current in many higher education contexts today. It would affect the ways in which the current assessment and feedback processes play out in the round. How then would the assessment and feedback ele-ments need to be orchestrated?

Orchestrating assessment and feedback

The ways in which the pattern of assessment and feedback needs to play out depends on how the 'audiences' are chosen. Enabling students to create some assessment outputs directed at designated audiences can once again involve a variety of approaches, suited to different con-texts. Examples include, ranging from the least to the most radical:

- Tutor nominates an imagined audience for a given task and asks students to write/present *as if* to that audience.

- Students collectively nominate a putative audience for existing assignments, and adjust form and language accordingly in their assignment.
- Individual students select an imagined audience and write/present as if to their nominated audience.
- Students write/present to a targeted online audience, inviting feedback online.
- Students write/present to a real audience, asynchronously (e.g. creating a multi-media package for a company, writing an edited text or resource for a publishing company; writing an academic article for a particular journal).
- Students set up a 'real time' opportunity to engage with an audience, for example student peers, alumni, a local interest group or employers' representatives.

Some of the more radical options might lead to a significant change in the assessment and feedback process cycle we looked at earlier in the chapter, in that audiences may be engaged in co-creating opportunities for both learning and assessment. Feedback would then be built much more authentically and immediately into the activity via dialogue as part of its development, perhaps in the manner of a designer responding to the interests of a client.

This approach allows for a greater emphasis on learning activities involving collaborative work and peer dialogue (see Chapter 8), and on student-tutor dialogue (whether in person or online), than in the traditional assessment cycle. Initial feedback on these assessments, which can include indicative marks or grades so that students know in broad terms how they are progressing, becomes an integral part of the learning process, rather than distanced in time from the learning as is often the case in the traditional sequence.

The sequence of activities starts to change. Students:

1. take a class and/or undertake independent learning (e.g. via a virtual learning environment, through wider reading or experiential learning), which from the start foregrounds the needs and interests of particular audiences;
2. engage in learning through dialogue and collaboration, such that constructive feedback from peers and tutor is built into the activities;
3. discuss assessment criteria as an intrinsic part of these learning activities, using formative peer assessment tasks to develop shared understandings of what is required;

4. orientate themselves towards an external audience and, where possible, work in partnership with representatives of that audience to develop their thinking and gain additional formative feedback;

5. work on the assessment task, in the knowledge that it will make an important contribution to the final Showcase Portfolio, by actively using feedback from a range of sources to inform its development;

6. receive a provisional mark for the task;

7. include the task in the final, curated, Showcase Portfolio at the end of the programme and await holistic, formal assessment of their overall achievement on the programme.

This approach offers an integrated, holistic and developmental approach to assessment, putting more emphasis on learning through dialogue and engagement than on technical assessment processes. The Showcase Portfolio, making a significant contribution to the final level of award, could require some re-working of current institutional practices (including regulations). It would rightly vary in emphasis across different disciplines. But it has the distinct advantage of giving students time to develop their expertise and become acculturated into a given academic and/or professional community before submitting a substantial part of their work. This enables students not only to become competent but also to gain a greater sense of autonomy as they oversee the whole learning journey and consider its relationship to their personal context and future direction of travel.

4 Challenges for departments

Changing approaches to assessment has the potential to change the rhythms and cultures of engagement within and even across departments. A department may start to change, however, by introducing just one or two outward-facing assessments. Over time, a review of the whole shape of the programme could then reform the rhythm of assessment-related activity across the whole length of the programme of study. There is no quick fix for this; programme teams would probably need to look ahead to the next 3–5 year period to see how future students might begin a programme with outward-facing assessments and a programme-level Showcase Portfolio running through its core. Changes may be needed at institutional level, for example with respect to assessment regulations and mechanisms for recording assessments across a whole programme, if the full changes recommended here are to be implemented. But the Connected Curriculum approach *is* about changing the larger direction of travel, for institutions and for the sector.

One valuable way of planning effective changes to curriculum is to work with students or student representatives, along with alumni, to co-create new curriculum design. This can also create a sense of human connection and belonging within a department and institution. We turn to the theme of human connections in Chapter 8, which addresses the final dimension of the Connected Curriculum framework: 'Students connect with each other, across phases and with alumni.'

5 Vignettes of practice

This set of vignettes illustrates ways in which students can learn and be assessed through producing outputs directed at an audience. The first two involve students in creating digital outputs. In the first, students produce digital communications for the public about London on the first year of a History degree at UCL and, in the second, students at the London School of Economics make films about international politics. The third outlines how students at the University of Sheffield produce a business report, and the fourth vignette shows how students at the University of Liverpool Management School undertake research and then report to a task group as part of the university's engagement strategy.

1. Making History: Engaging the public with insights into the history of London in the UCL Department of History through digital outputs

Working in a small team, first-year students on the Making History module produce a presentation, in person and using digital media, explaining the historical significance of an object or place. They are challenged to understand the object or place, contextualise it and tell its story. Why was it created? How has it been used? Has its meaning changed?

Making History encourages students to be self-reflective about History as a discipline and as a practice. New media such as electronic forms of communication, television, films and websites are raising new questions about historical methodologies and the politics of the preservation of historical sources. In response to this, students are asked to focus on historical process and method as much as on producing an historical product. How as a group they arrive at their

(Continued)

final website and presentation is as important as what they ultimately conclude in response to their chosen research question.

Each website and each final presentation is awarded a single assessment mark, which is shared by each member of the group. Accordingly, each member of the group assumes equal responsibility for ensuring that the project is completed on time and to a high standard. Learning to work effectively as a group is one of the key skills Making History is designed to develop. Students also learn to apply assessment criteria fairly to the work of others on this module, as part of the assessment of the group presentations.

The presentations are aimed at an intelligent, but non-specialist, public audience and involve two or three digital outputs. Whatever students produce should take no longer than 20 minutes to read, listen to or view, but the forms they can use are varied. Examples of digital outputs include a website providing information in an interactive way, a podcast, a video or an interactive map, diagram, or image. Assessment criteria include successfully communicating historical ideas and concepts including, where appropriate and helpful, historiography, to a general audience.

Vignette submitted by Dr Adam Smith, Senior Lecturer in the UCL Department of History.

2. Visual International Politics at London School of Economics

International Relations is in the midst of a 'visual turn', because images play an increasingly important role in shaping international political events and our understanding of them. 'Visual International Politics', a final-year undergraduate course at the London School of Economics, is unique because students don't just study and critique visual media – they make their own films. The course thus has conceptual and practical objectives and so employs pedagogies of metacognition and experiential learning in order to achieve those.

At a conceptual level, students learn how to use a range of theoretical and methodological approaches to interpret photographs, films and other visual media. The course also has practical objectives: it is the only International Relations course that provides practice-based training in documentary filmmaking. Students thus learn to 'think visually' by interpreting images and making films, and there is a demonstrable, mutual benefit to both their textual and visual practices as a result.

In 2015–16, for example, students' ten-minute documentary films addressed such diverse topics as the global politics of beards ('Beard Goggles'), a behind-the-scenes look at London's Russian elite ('Bliny vs. Scones'), and a political ethnography of London's nighttime economy and its workers ('The Night Bus').

Visual International Politics is part of the wider 'Students as Producers' initiative at LSE, which aims to deliver improvements to learning outcomes by diversifying assessment and recognising students as co-creators and co-producers of knowledge. The course receives enthusiastic feedback from students, who value it both for its uniquely critical approach and for providing valuable transferable skills.

Vignette submitted by William A. Callahan, Professor of International Relations and Darren Moon, Senior Learning Technologist, LSE. The students' films can be seen at https://vimeo.com/channels/IR318

3. Enquiry-based assessment in a Business Intelligence module at the University of Sheffield: Developing a Business Report

The final-year undergraduate module in Business Intelligence offered by the University of Sheffield Information School is assessed through an innovative, enquiry-based collaborative business report combined with two pieces of reflective writing, one about their experiences of working as a group and one reflecting on their information literacy development.

The module focuses on the ways in which business people use information and on how external information is used to inform business strategy and create competitive advantage. It can be difficult to understand these information activities in organisations, particularly if students lack work experience. The coursework enables them to understand at a much deeper level the information gathering, evaluation, synthesis and presentation activities that business people undertake.

The collaborative, enquiry-based activity involves students working in small teams to investigate the business information needs of a Business Partner – a 'real life' information problem. I work with University of Sheffield Enterprise to source local business people who want to work with students. Because of this many of the business partners are recent startups, social enterprises or even entrepreneurs with ideas. This messy, unstructured real world enquiry allows students to develop problem-solving skills and provides a bridge from the safe world of academic assignments to the more open and unsure world of business.

(Continued)

Students form self-selecting groups of three to five members. This flexibility with group size allows students to take control over who they choose to work with; this seems to improve group functionality. In addition, students receive support sessions to discuss group-working protocols, the value of group working for skills development, communication, group roles and positive outcomes from group work.

Students are provided with a very short project brief before they have the opportunity to interview their business partner about their information needs. The experience of meeting business people outside of the context of a job interview is very powerful and many groups go on to produce excellent, well-researched business reports for their partners. The two reflective assignments (20 per cent each of the module mark) mitigate the potentially negative effect of having group work in the final, important year of undergraduate studies. Through the reflective writing students become more aware of their own roles in groups and can more easily identify what they could do in the future to improve communication, collaboration and problem solving. Their information literacy development, a key skill for lifelong learning, becomes explicit through the reflective process. The business report requires students to collaborate on presenting findings to a specific audience, focusing their attention on appropriate modes of communication as well as developing their information literacy.

Submitted by Pamela McKinney, Lecturer, Information School, University of Sheffield.

4. Students on a Sustainability in Business module at the University of Liverpool Management School report to a Task Group

The University of Liverpool Management School runs an innovative module that embeds information and digital literacies through an enquiry-based learning approach. The topic of the module is sustainability in business, a very current issue that demands online research as emerging practices and ideas may not yet appear in the print literature. The module is run as a series of team-based workshops.

There are a number of outcomes from the workshop activities, such as editing a Wikipedia article related to sustainability and providing reports to inform university sustainability activities. This requires the students to develop a high level of information literacy and, key to this, is the enhancement of their digital literacies; these are closely linked with their academic skill sets and patterns of practice. The students practise advanced search techniques for a variety of search tools and develop skills in managing data, for example through using online referencing tools.

Once data from a variety of sources have been collected, students are shown how to perform methodical analysis using a variety of electronic tools to facilitate critical evaluation. For example, they are exposed to content analysis and thematic analysis, very useful approaches to the critical analysis of a body of literature. These are demonstrated and supported through the use of digital tools such as MindGenius or NVivo. Team members are also encouraged to develop skills in using digital tools for collaboration and facilitation, including tools on our university virtual learning environment and social networking tools such as Facebook and Twitter.

Primary data collection in the form of interviews – a key source of information in the business environment – is an important element in this module. Students have been able to explore issues of interest with leading figures in the corporate sustainability community. Currently students are linking with Planning students from the Department of Geography in a University-wide project on Green Spaces. They perform a management evaluation of the Planning students' proposals to the University Green Space Task Group and then report to this task group as part of the university's engagement strategy. This will necessitate interviewing the Planning students about their reports.

Student engagement in this module has been high. Module and focus group feedback confirmed that students did gain important skills in digital scholarship, group working and reflection in addition to subject-specific skills. A number of students from the module volunteered to become Digital Champions. They acted as peer-learning facilitators to first-year students, advising them on digital tools and strategies for their research-based assignments. This demonstrates the impact of the sustainability module on students' learning and also the confidence they have gained through undertaking research and enquiry and producing outputs for a targeted audience.

Submitted by Simon Snowden, Tünde Varga-Atkins and Emma Thompson from the University of Liverpool. An earlier version of the module is written up as a JISC case study: http://digitalstudent.jisc-involve.org/wp/files/2015/01/DS23-Integrating-digital-literacy-with-enquiry-based-learning.pdf

8
Connecting students with one another and with alumni

1 Connecting with others

The sixth dimension of the Connected Curriculum framework 'Students connect with each other, across phases and with alumni focuses on the importance of human connections. It highlights the intellectual value for students of participating with their diverse peers in collaborative enquiry and the personal benefits of studying in a supportive community, for example via mentor schemes or connecting with alumni.

Why do these human connections matter? Making connections with other people, with their varying backgrounds and perspectives is important for at least three reasons. First, it contributes to the development of students' learning and especially to their critical thinking skills. Second, working and meeting with other students and alumni builds active networks, creating a sense of belonging to a community and helping to prepare students for the complex social demands of life and the workplace. More fundamentally for the Connected Curriculum initiative, learning with and from others is more than just part of the educational process: it is the *goal* of education. If we accept that education is rightly directed towards the common good, and is not just a set of opportunities for competitive individual advancement, its purpose might be defined as creating and sustaining productive human connections and collaborations. In this chapter we look first at a range of practical ways of achieving these human connections within and beyond the planned curriculum and then at the educational principles underpinning this approach. We conclude with our final set of vignettes of practice.

2 Practical approaches

How might we review the planned curriculum to ensure that it provides suitable opportunities for students to benefit from making connections with others? Table 8.1 offers a range of possibilities to promote discussion among departments and programme teams about whether any additional activities might be valuable in the local context.

Although this table focuses on undergraduate students, many of the same ideas can be used for students on taught postgraduate programmes. Peer study groups, mentoring schemes (with mentors drawn, for example, from the department's postgraduate research students) and meetings with alumni are all equally relevant to Masters students. Some of these examples are teaching and assessment methods, while others are informal. We will look at each of these briefly in turn.

3 Collaborative learning and groups assessments

Why ask students to work in groups and to collaborate as they learn? There has been a strong focus in higher education on independent working, at the expense of learning how to work interdependently and, as Bruffee (1999) argues, collaboration has been seen as something to be frowned upon rather than promoted. Yet working collaboratively 'teaches students to work together effectively when the stakes are relatively low, so that they can work together effectively later when the stakes are high' (Bruffee 1999, xiii).

Although some students will immediately take to collaborative tasks, others will find it particularly challenging, especially if they are not accustomed to it. However, if managed well and if students are given time to build up their group-related confidence and skills, setting students up to work together can have multiple advantages. The following are commonly identified:

- developing higher order thinking skills;
- building self-esteem;
- developing a range of communication skills;
- developing confidence and skills in the digital domain;
- encouraging understanding of diversity;
- developing collaborative problem-solving approaches.

Table 8.1 Promoting productive personal connections: some ideas for practice

Who connects?	With whom?	How?	For what purpose?
Students on arrival at university	Immediate peers	• Personal/academic tutorial group, using prompt questions to guide conversations • Timetabled small group meetings linked to collaborative investigative task (e.g. Meet the Researcher: see Chapter 3) • Online investigative peer group activity • Online discussion groups	• Helping with transition (e.g. from school or workplace) • Building good working relationships • Cultivating a collaborative, investigative culture from day one • Setting expectations of regular engagement
	Established students	• Social events • Online social networking • Mentoring scheme	• Help develop sense of belonging • Establish habits of engagement • Provide ongoing support
Established undergraduate students	Immediate peers	• Seminars and tutorial groups • Timetabled peer study groups, where 5–6 students meet (not roomed – i.e. students have to meet informally or online) to work on a set learning task, which can be reported on via tutorial groups or via virtual learning environment (e.g. discussion forum)	• Develop good, collaborative working relationships • Enable students to explore new topics together without tutor present, to prepare for and/or follow up on classes • Promote a culture of peer support • Help overcome perceived barriers due to difference in background
	Senior peers on same degree	• Working together on collaborative assessments (e.g. projects, wikis, presentations, curating digital resources)	• Co-develop new skills, e.g. planning a presentation, using new software applications • Raise awareness of ongoing opportunity for

Peers on a degree programme in different discipline	• Mentoring • Students as teachers: e.g. second-year students help to teach key concepts to first years, in person or online, which enables them to consolidate own learning	• Highlight need to consolidate new knowledge over time and share with others in future • Extend intellectual gaze beyond own discipline(s)
Postgraduate students	• Collaborate on interdisciplinary task/assessment, or on an extra-curricular activity • Undergraduate students attend informal seminar series in which postgraduate students present on their research	• Make new personal connections beyond own department • Raise awareness of importance of undergraduate research
Alumni	• Undergraduates shadow postgraduate researchers for a day	• Offer insights into how disciplinary knowledge is explored and extended through research
Alumni and peers	• Departmental meeting with successful alumni, encouraging active engagement • Undergraduate students organise an event/conference to showcase their work/research	• Stimulate self-belief and raise awareness of future possibilities • Motivate students to engage; build skills and confidence; provide opportunity for feedback on work.

In addition, by working in cooperative groups, students learn to express themselves in the language of their subject discipline, and even develop stronger links with academic staff (Jaques 2000).

There are inevitably challenges associated with working in groups. There may be practical barriers: it is can be hard for students to collaborate in a banked lecture theatre, or when opportunities cannot be found in the timetable for them to meet and work together, although online discussion facilities may help here. Working collaboratively stretches students, emulating the kinds of real-world tasks undertaken in the workplace. Research suggests that lecturers need to be aware of both the benefits and challenges for students of working with peers with culturally and linguistically diverse backgrounds (Moore and Hampton 2015). Effective working in diverse groups may be conditional on teachers preparing, coaching and debriefing students about the expected benefits associated with group work throughout the course (Sweeney, Weaven and Herington 2008).

Particular attention needs to be given to fairness in the design of the assessed group work, especially in designing transparent criteria for allocating marks (Caple and Bogle 2013). Although new technologies and 'big data' have potential for allocating marks more fairly (Williams 2016), allocating half the weighting in a collaborative task to a shared-group mark and the other half to a personal mark based on the individual's specific contribution may be a pragmatic approach. Again, virtual learning environments can be helpful here. For example, individual students' contributions to a wiki can be tracked and their contributions to the research for, and preparation of, a group presentation can be seen via an online collaborative forum.

Enabling students to provide and respond constructively to peer assessment and feedback (Nicol and Macfarlane-Dick 2006; Falchikov 2007; Carnell 2016) is another challenge but, undertaken with sensitivity, it can greatly enhance students' understandings of the expectations of the discipline. These understandings and skills are applicable to multiple contexts, including the workplace (Chapter 6).

The specific challenges of group work and collaborative assessments can certainly be seen as opportunities in a research-based curriculum. These activities afford opportunities for students to investigate *how* groups work and what the barriers are to effective collaborative practices (Jaques 2000). Students can be challenged to discuss related issues of equality and made aware of how research has highlighted the marginalisation of certain groups in social settings.

To create time in any one module or unit, for students both to take on a group project, including peer assessment *and* to investigate the skills challenges and benefits of these activities, is a challenge; this is where once again, the value of a connected throughline of enquiry-based activities can be very helpful. Carefully designed, such a deliberate sequence of activities can sustain a focus on these issues throughout the programme. And if a programme-wide portfolio is ultimately employed, students can reflect analytically on what and how they have learned when collaborating with peers, as part of the curated presentation of their work.

4 Connecting beyond the curriculum

What is the status of activities undertaken by students beyond the taught curriculum? Students may for example take up optional co-curricular activities, such as engagement with a student society, a volunteering activity or the opportunity to lead an educational change project. Promoting such opportunities at appropriate points in the programme can be very helpful, building students' sense of belonging.

The lived environment again plays a part here; where students have easy accessibility to shared, comfortable spaces, they can build connections informally. However, there are typically great demands on physical spaces with rising student numbers and, of course, some students learn off campus (if there is a campus), and even at a considerable distance from the home institution. In these cases, many departments are finding innovative ways of building a sense of community. Shared flagship events or field trips, for example, can be invaluable, especially early in a programme so that students get to know one another more quickly.

Student cohorts can also build a strong sense of engagement and identity through online social networking. It is useful for departments to keep up-to-date with current guidance on possible options (see UCISA 2015). There can be a tension between requiring students to engage, for example, in a discussion forum on an institutional virtual learning environment and encouraging them to cultivate their own social networking groups. There is no single 'one size fits all' solution but engaging students in discussions about what works best for them right now can be useful: this is likely to change fairly quickly, with the changing popularity of social networking platforms, so an open atmosphere whereby everyone can share their ideas is invaluable.

A department adopting a Showcase Portfolio approach (Chapter 7) can in principle invite students to reflect analytically on dimensions of their wider experience as part of the final portfolio, if it suits the disciplinary context. However, some students can more readily access these co-curricular or extra-curricular activities than others. Some arrive at university laden with economic, social and cultural capital; they may have, for example, sufficient resources not to need to undertake paid work, and the confidence borne of a particular kind of family and educational background. Other students may not have the time, confidence or inclination to take up extra-curricular opportunities. So putting too much store in any assessment scheme on rewarding students for going 'above and beyond' that which is required in the curriculum needs to be thought about carefully. However, a Showcase Portfolio can be a useful stimulus for connecting students across phases of study – for example, by inviting first-year students to become an audience for final year showcase presentations, whether in real time or online.

5 Working with alumni

It is worth revisiting the benefits, as well as the challenges, of maintaining links with alumni and of continuing to include them in the life of the department and institution. Of course by no means all alumni will either want to or be in a position to sustain a meaningful relationship with their institution, but some can and do. Across the higher education sector, there has been growing activity targeting alumni as financial donors, and, ethically undertaken, this can provide a valuable source of funding for the benefit of new students, especially those who may particularly need financial support. But there are other ways in which alumni can be invited to stay involved. Alumni can be invited to:

- Visit the department to encourage students to engage with their studies, for example by recalling their own learning experiences and outlining the ways in which the programme has influenced them in the workplace and in life more broadly.
- Promote further opportunities within the department, for example by talking to undergraduates about their experiences of postgraduate study.
- Attend selected departmental-level events, such as guest lectures, and participate in related discussions.
- Become involved in the development of high-profile events, such as an undergraduate research conference or a research-related poster competition.
- Act as a mentor for students in relation to a specific activity in the curriculum, such as interdisciplinary problem-solving tasks or independent research projects.

- Act as an adviser for student mentors, for example by speaking at a developmental event for mentors.
- Play a role in connecting students with audiences and partners for their outward-facing assessments.
- Take on the role of partner in helping the department to develop its educational provision (for example, enhancing curriculum content and design) and its wider provision (for example, developing a cross-cohort mentor scheme).

Within the limits of what is practical, enabling students to make links with alumni, even intermittently, can enrich their learning in many ways. Students will also know that, when they have graduated, the departmental and institutional communities remain open to them.

6 The value and values of human connections in education

Why should it matter if students connect with one another when they study? It is perfectly possible to argue that learning is a solo sport: that it is the individual who does the learning, who ultimately gets assessed on that learning and who receives an award. Learning can certainly happen when alone, for example through interaction with objects, and it has been quite common for academic literature on learning and teaching in higher education to see learning in terms of individual students engaging with their 'object of study':

> Learning is about experiencing the object of study in a different way, where the experience is a relationship between the person experiencing and the object experienced. (Prosser and Trigwell 1999, 13)

However, a number of arguments can be set against this. First, a focus on human connections foregrounds the need to create an environment in which students participate as fully and actively in their studies as possible, rather than just assuming a passive role out on the edge. It speaks to raising students' levels of overall engagement, and:

> Engagement does not simply equate to the amount of involvement in and time on task, important though that is. It extends to learners' engagement in communities of practice, to their involvement in a variety of networks and to the amount and quality of interchanges with others. (Knight 2002, 275)

We need to create spaces for such engagement, rather than filling up every corner of the curriculum with individual tasks. Barnett and Coate (2005) argue that there is a difference between 'operational engagement', whereby a student is getting on with a set activity, and the kind of engagement whereby she or he becomes fully, personally, authentically engaged:

> She engages with the task in hand – with other students, with the problem, with the particular challenge – because she aligns herself to it wholeheartedly. She wills herself *into* the task. She tackles it with enthusiasm, with élan, with imagination. ... She and the task – in this moment – are one. It is *her* task. There is, in such an instance, a unity in being and learning. (Barnett and Coate 2005, 138–139)

Will all students experience this kind of engagement, all of the time? No. But understanding that learning is part of a deeper sense of self – as Barnett and Coate argue, that it is made up of knowing, acting *and* being – may help departments and students orientate themselves even more actively towards creating a curriculum in which personal engagement is specifically cultivated. Curriculum, defined in this way, is more than subject content, intended learning outcomes and taught classes. It is:

> curriculum-in-action, which is the interplay of all those involved. (2005, 159)

And active engagement helps to prepare students to have agency in the world.

But the argument for human connections reaches beyond issues of engagement to the nature of learning itself. Sociocultural and social constructivist theories, developed by leading figures such as Vygotsky, Piaget and Bruner, point to the socially situated nature of new understandings; what we learn, and how we express and act on what we know, is profoundly affected by interaction with others. For Bruner, learning is not a solitary act. He highlights the extent to which meanings are constructed not just through solitary thought and engagement with the object of study but by means of 'interpersonal negotiation':

> Meaning is what we can agree upon or at least accept as a working basis for seeking agreement about the concept in hand. (Bruner 1986, 122)

Bruner argues that 'most learning in most settings is a communal activity, a sharing of the culture' (1986, 127) and that 'Social realities are not bricks that we trip over or bruise ourselves on when we kick at them, but the meanings that we achieve by the sharing of human cognition' (1986, 122). Geertz argues similarly that:

> Human thought is consummately social: social in its origins, social in its functions, social in its forms and social in its applications. (Geertz 1973, 360)

Of course, there are academic arguments contesting the extent to which knowledge is socially constructed: is there no foundational knowledge, nothing we can rely on? Bruffee (1999), in his work on collaborative learning in the humanities, rejects the idea that there is, or ever could be, a fixed and certain body of knowledge that students need to learn. Drawing on scholars such as Dewey, Rorty and Latour, he also cites Thomas Kuhn (1970), whose work on the structure of scientific revolutions highlighted historic shifts in scientific thinking and knowing. But, as we saw in Chapter 2, the term 'research' is conceived differently across and even within different disciplines; there are many who reject the relativist position described above, and are committed to the rigour of scientific method. Yet historians and philosophers of science continue to ask important questions, for example about the ways in which scientific knowledge changes over time and the cultural factors affecting its reception by society. Is scientific knowledge entirely independent of subjective human judgement? What is the relationship between observation and interpretation? Is the language used to communicate knowledge transparent or can it be value-laden? How is scientific research affected by structures of power and systemic inequalities in our society?

These are just some of the countless questions that can be asked about the nature of research, about what 'good' research is and about what it makes sense to say that we know, under what circumstances. The questions are nuanced and multi-layered. But this is the very strength of higher education: right across the sector, experts of every kind are shedding light on the synergies and contradictions of our emerging understandings of the world. To draw students explicitly into this rich landscape of dialogue, inviting them to investigate and to test evidence and argument, is to engage them in high-quality, research-based education. Collaborating with peers and connecting with alumni acculturates students into this dialogic space, prompting them to see not only through others' eyes but also to see things more clearly through their own.

Research-based curriculum, well designed, can challenge diverse students to enquire, to test, to visit others who experience the world differently. It can prompt students to consider their own position in relation to the reliability of knowledge, its complexities and its edges. It can even foster new critical debate among academics, professionals and communities, fostering an intellectual energy that sparks new approaches to research and its application to the world.

In many respects, the sixth is the most straightforward of the dimensions of the Connected Curriculum framework. Promoting human connections, the building of productive relationships, may seem like an obvious aim. But in another sense it is perhaps the most profound. Higher education institutions are complex communities, with growing numbers of students and an increasingly diverse student body; it is not always easy for students to feel as if they belong or as if there is space for them to express themselves in the learning and research community they have joined. Designing a curriculum in which spaces are created explicitly for students to engage with others' perspectives, including unfamiliar conceptions of knowledge, is both an intellectual and a values-based endeavour. This dimension of the Connected Curriculum reminds us that:

> [W]hile education is an ongoing process of improving knowledge and skills, it is also – perhaps primarily – an exceptional means of bringing about personal development and building relationships among individuals, groups and nations. (Delors/UNESCO 1996, 12)

7 Vignettes of practice

In our last set of vignettes, departments describe ways in which they are purposefully enabling students to connect with one another, across year groups, phases and disciplines, and with alumni. In the first vignette, students on different modern language degrees link up with museum collections to curate an exhibition. In the second, students connect with students from different year groups by participating in their own undergraduate research conference. The third vignette describes how students are benefiting from cross-year tutorial groups in Biomedical Engineering, and the fourth describes an innovative approach in Physics that enables students to produce videos on complex concepts for future students. The final vignette outlines an initiative that enables medical and pharmacy students to connect across a number of London hospitals.

1. Scandinavian Collections: Joint Danish and Norwegian Language Classes in the UCL Art Museum

Despite the similarities between the languages, students of Danish and Norwegian have often struggled to communicate with one another each using their language of study. Given the close ties between the countries, being able to navigate both languages in spoken and written form is an advantage that increases their readiness for employment. In 2015 we therefore established a collaboration with the UCL Art Museum and UCL Special Collections with the aim of combining joint Danish and Norwegian classes with research-based learning.

Through research and archival work, we compiled a list of Scandinavian items that are part of UCL's Collections. These items ranged from the engravings of illustrations used in a nineteenth-century travel book on Norway to documents relating to Scandinavian journeys undertaken by former UCL staff members. We then designed three joint Danish and Norwegian classes for each language year-group, an assessed project and an exhibition. During the classes all groups had to concentrate, though to a different extent depending on their language proficiency, on the description of the objects, the role of the museum and the intercultural connections between the UK and Scandinavia.

For the assessed project the students selected a Scandinavian object in the UCL Special Collections and conducted their own individual research. The students were also collectively responsible for curating the final exhibition and preparing all the exhibition materials in both languages. The exhibition, part of the UCL Festival of Culture, allowed the students to present their research on Anglo-Scandinavian history to academic and non-academic audiences.

The students of both languages embraced the project and showed a genuine interest in exploring the forgotten connections between UCL and Scandinavia. Working on these activities outside the classroom gave them the opportunity to use their language to discuss original case studies and created a greater sense of group dynamic across language and year groups. These, in turn, minimised difficulties in Danish-Norwegian intercommunication. Seeing students communicating about these objects, overcoming the issues that, in a traditional classroom context, are often perceived as language barriers, was extremely satisfying both for us and the students.

Vignette submitted by Dr Elettra Carbone (Senior Teaching Fellow) and Jesper Hansen (Senior Teaching Fellow), UCL.

2. The Student Biochemistry & Molecular Biology Conference at UCL

In 2013–14, we established the inaugural UCL Biochemistry & Molecular Biology Conference, an annual event that has been explicitly designed to provide a comprehensive and realistic research experience. It engages final-year research project students in the post-research process of presenting their work at a formal research conference as part of their assessment.

Previously students participated in a single week-long session of oral presentations but now students submit abstracts of their work in advance and these must be approved by their academic supervisor. These are triaged into specific presentation areas and the student talks are run at parallel presentation sessions over a single afternoon. This gives students the opportunity to enhance their critical reasoning skills. Liaising with their supervisors to discuss abstract submissions and presentations, they are introduced to the process of collaborative endeavour required to generate research outputs. They are then assessed by directing these outputs to an audience.

Student and staff engagement with the conference is excellent. Undergraduate students from years one and two attend the talks and this enables them to engage in the research process at all levels of the curriculum. The undergraduate research conference closes at a reception where the best student presentation receives prize monies from industrial sponsors who have attended the sessions and participated in the judging. These innovations provide students with an enjoyable opportunity to present their work to an audience and participate in a learning experience that is closely allied to the academic research experience. Staff enjoy the opportunity to provide a learning experience that is more closely allied to the academic research experience and future employers are engaged in teaching and assessment.

Submitted by Prof Andrea Townsend-Nicholson, Prof Elizabeth Shephard and Suzanne Ruddy, UCL.

3. Tutorials enabling Students to Connect across Year Groups in Biomedical Engineering

Tutorials provide an opportunity for students to reflect on their learning, make holistic connections between modules and see their subject in a broad context. We have restructured the tutorials in our Biomedical Engineering programme so that each tutorial group includes students from all years of the programme. The main reason for this change was to encourage students to connect between year groups so that newer students can learn from more experienced near-peers and so that students reaching the end of their programme can recognise how much they have learned and matured.

This approach gives practical help to newer students by involving established students in tackling the problems they face, allowing them to form their own support groups organically without the commitment required by a formal mentoring programme. Pedagogically, we aim to use tutorials to emphasise continuity throughout the degree, enabling students to form connections between their learning year-by-year, and to see how their understanding and expertise develops through the programme.

An initial feedback questionnaire suggested that students in the later years of their degree felt that they would gain less from this scheme than new students. We have tackled this concern by scheduling tutorials to ensure that each session contains material relevant to all students and by retaining year-group tutorials in cases where there is material that is only relevant to one year group. An additional benefit is that the tutor's role increasingly becomes one of facilitating problem solving between students. This means that the tutor needs less programme-specific knowledge, allowing a broader range of staff to get involved in tutoring.

We are reviewing the new tutorial system by monitoring students' feedback with questionnaires, which we will use to refine our approach as the programme develops.

Vignette submitted by Adam Gibson, Professor of Medical Physics, UCL.

4. The 'Physics concept' video at UCL

Students working in small teams are asked to make a short video to explain a concept from one of their Physics modules that they themselves have found difficult. The best videos are then passed to the lecturer for the relevant module to be included as part of the online resources for that course.

It is known that learning through teaching can be valuable, and here the students are revisiting material from other modules that they found

(Continued)

challenging, as well as learning it well enough to teach it. In addition, future cohorts can benefit from the material generated because more videos, useful to a range of modules, are produced every year.

Allowing the students to choose the topics that were difficult for them provides the lecturers with insights into which aspects students are struggling with, as well as mitigating the problem in future years by providing specifically targeted resources. With the students producing these resources, it also lessens the load on the lecturer.

Another benefit from this piece of coursework is the social aspect. Students are in small randomly assigned groups of around four, so they work with people they might not have known before. This task is run early in the course for this reason – to try to provide for the students a group they feel they belong to and can go to if they have any problems on the course.

The marking of the coursework is largely based on the question of whether the video would help other students struggling with that topic or not, as that was the aim, but includes criteria relating to whether other students are likely to remember what the video has taught them. Creativity is strongly encouraged! For this reason, only a small quota of marks is given to the 'technical accomplishment' of the videos although, in cases where the technical accomplishment aids the teaching (for example, where animations are used to explain something more clearly than could be achieved with diagrams), then higher marks can be given for the work they have produced.

The outcomes of this piece of coursework are excellent. Students embrace the chance to unleash their creativity and some very useful and memorable teaching videos have been created. The students on the whole enjoy the project and the chance to showcase any artistic talent, with most of them appreciating the opportunity to work in groups. Success!

Vignette submitted by Elinor Bailey, Teaching Fellow at UCL.

5. 'Be the Change': pan-London Medical School Initiative

'Be the Change' was a new initiative piloted in 2015–16, launched with the aim of empowering medical and pharmacy students to become healthcare leaders, both of today and the future. During this pilot year, the initiative ran as a pan-London medical school competition, where teams from each medical school competed to develop the best portfolio of student-led quality improvement projects.

As part of the larger UCL team, our specific project was to assess whether a virtual reality mobile phone simulator (*Touch Surgery*) could be a useful educational adjunct for medical students learning clinical skills procedures. We went on to test this hypothesis by running a randomised medical education trial, and the project subsequently developed into something much more substantial than we were initially expecting! Nevertheless, as a new student-led initiative, we faced significant challenges without formal funding or previous academic credence. Therefore, to ensure the success of the project, and to highlight the viability of student-led initiatives for the future, we were required to independently recruit experts in statistics, clinical skills and medical education. In addition, as a 'pop-up' group, we had to search for money from unconventional funding sources (e.g. medical leadership organisations, conference competitions). Despite these challenges, the project was an overall success and we managed to recruit nearly 30 students into the trial. Our results showed that virtual reality simulators did not have the same efficacy as gold-standard educational resources, yet they were markedly better than students repetitively practising procedures on the wards alone. This was a significant finding, since gold-standard clinical skills training resources are not always available to medical students whilst on hospital placements, and mobile phone simulators are freely available to students at all times. Ultimately, our project showed the viability of a well-supported, student-led and student-delivered medical education initiative. And, along with the rest of the UCL team, we went on to win first prize in the overall 'Be the Change' competition.

Submitted by Richard D. Bartlett, MBPhD medical student at UCL researching tissue-engineered therapies for spinal cord repair, and project leader of one of the student-led UCL 'Be the Change' projects.

9
A Connected Curriculum
at UCL

1 Institutional context

This chapter outlines the ways in which the flexible Connecte
Curriculum framework has been introduced to UCL in the UK as pa
of a wider institutional strategy. UCL's intention is to build on, exter
and celebrate established areas of good practice across the institutio
The Connected Curriculum, with its core principle that students lea
through research and enquiry and its six related dimensions, is becor
ing a catalyst for dialogue among faculty members, professional sta
students and alumni.

UCL is a large, research-intensive university based in centr
London. It was founded in 1826 as a secular alternative to Oxford a
Cambridge. Now with nearly 40,000 students, it comprises a very wi
range of academic disciplines and professions, ranging from Fine Art
Physics, from Architecture to Medicine, and from Classics to Comput
Science. It is particularly known for its research. Its research 'inte
sity' was evidenced in the UK's 2014 Research Excellence Framewo
research evaluation exercise, where it was the top-rated university
the UK for research strength, by a measure of average research sco
multiplied by staff numbers submitted (UCL 2016c). More than half
UCL's students are postgraduates, which makes its profile unusual.
eleven Faculties have a considerable degree of autonomy, with very d
tinctive cultures and histories.

How did the Connected Curriculum initiative at UCL come ir
being? In the summer of 2013, Professor Michael Arthur took up t
post of UCL President and Provost. His appointment heralded a n
focus on raising the quality of student education in the institution

mirror that of its research and on building synergies between the two. During the academic year 2013–14, a series of events, seminars, 'town hall' discussions and online consultations at UCL engaged academics, professional staff, students and other stakeholders in discussion about UCL's values and mission. This led to the development and publication of a 20-year strategy, 'UCL 2034' (UCL 2016d). Its key objectives include 'addressing global challenges through our disciplinary excellence and distinctive cross-disciplinary approach'; developing as 'an accessible, publicly-engaged organization that fosters a lifelong community'; and 'delivering global impact through a network of innovative international activities, collaborations and partnerships'.

The section of the UCL 2034 strategy articulating intentions for student education focuses on UCL becoming 'A global leader in the integration of research and education, underpinning an inspirational student experience':

> We will inspire our students at every level – undergraduate, postgraduate taught and postgraduate research – and equip them with the knowledge and skills that they need to contribute significantly to society and be leaders of the future in their chosen field and profession. All our students and staff will be seen as collaborative members of our university community, with a shared interest in the future of UCL.
>
> Our students will participate in the research process and the creation of knowledge, supported by our academic and research staff. They will understand the 'edge of knowledge' and learn how to deal with uncertainty. Through this integrated approach, they will develop their critical independent thinking skills, become confident problem solvers, be well-versed in communicating complex information and experienced at working in a team. With these skills, our graduates will excel in the workplace and be highly valued contributors across all walks of life.
>
> (UCL 2016d: Integration of research and education)

Playing a key role as a catalyst for taking forward these ambitions was the UCL Centre for Advancing Learning and Teaching (CALT), now known as the Arena Centre for Research-based Education. I am the academic Director of this department, working directly to the Vice Provost for Education and Student Affairs, Professor Anthony Smith. The UCL Arena Centre for Research-based Education aims to:

- ensure that the university offers the best possible quality of education for its students, by forging creative connections between its world-leading research and its teaching and learning at all levels of the curriculum, and by enabling students to learn through participating in research;

- provide authentic opportunities for all faculty members and professional staff who teach, support students' learning and/or are leaders of education to develop their teaching and educational leadership practices, and to gain appropriate qualifications;
- work with students as partners, encouraging them to be leaders and makers of change;
- influence and contribute to the higher education sector nationally and internationally in relation to the development of research-based higher education, academic practice and academic leadership.

Comprising Senior and Principal Teaching Fellows with different kinds of disciplinary and educational expertise as well as professional staff, the Arena Centre liaises with faculty members to develop student education in ways that suit different disciplines and curriculum levels. The team also undertakes education-focused scholarly research; we aim to draw on evidence-informed research in all projects and activities. We offer modest amounts of funding to UCL's Faculties for innovative developments, allocated through competitive bidding schemes. Regularly welcoming visitors from across UCL and from the wider national and international higher education community for discussions and events, we collaborate on numerous developmental projects.

In my role as Academic Director, I worked closely with Vice Provost Professor Anthony Smith to develop a way of framing discussions about new approaches to enhancing student education particularly, but not exclusively, through connecting students with research. The intention was to share existing good practice and to stimulate creative thinking across the range of diverse disciplines and contexts, about how we could ensure that all students had regular opportunities to benefit from studying in a research-rich environment. This means thinking about the ways in which programmes of study, both undergraduate and postgraduate are designed; it also means looking again at the wider culture of departments and Faculties in which students are studying. The intention is also to shine a light on cross-institutional features and systems that need to be improved. These include physical learning spaces, online administrative systems and academic regulations. We work closely with other UCL departments, such as Digital Education and Academic Services, to join up opportunities, challenges and solutions.

The senior leadership team is always keen to work in partnership with students and their representatives, and the relationship between the institution and the student union, UCLU, has been steadily strengthened. The UK National Student Survey (NSS), which asks students about their experience across a number of themes, including teaching, assessment and feedback, and academic support, has also been helpful. We have been able to draw on student feedback data from this and other surveys to understand better where our students are getting a great experience and where there are aspects of educational provision that needed to be improved.

2 Strategic introduction of the Connected Curriculum

Following a number of discussions and events, which drew together academics, professional colleagues and student representatives, the current set of six curriculum-related principles, or dimensions of practice, was developed. Presented in the form of the 'flower' graphic (Figure 1.1, shown again here), these dimensions drew on but extended ideas in relation to the concept of a 'Connected Curriculum' I had developed earlier in my career.

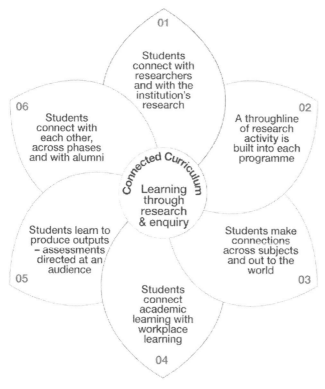

In 2014, UCL's Education Committee and then its senior Academic Committee formally approved the enhancement framework. Additional funding was made available for the appointments of two additional members of staff in the Arena Centre, who have taken a lead on the Connected Curriculum project, and to appoint a Visiting Professor, Mick Healey, who has brought valuable external advice and guidance. A Connected Curriculum Steering Group was created, which reports to the institution's central Education Committee, and a number of working groups began to invite colleagues and student representatives from across the institution to focus on different strands of activity. Membership of the groups remains open; we are keen that they are inclusive of both academic and professional staff, and that they promote student participation.

A range of introductory resources was developed to promote dialogue and the sharing of good practice in relation to the principles. The UCL Teaching and Learning Portal (UCL 2016e) began publishing case studies of existing good practice so that colleagues from across the institution could draw on the inspiration and experience of those in other disciplines. Further resources have been developed including a booklet with a programme evaluation grid (UCL 2016f). This is intended to help departments, programme teams and students discuss how well developed their own programmes already are in relation to each of the six dimensions and to make reasonable plans for further improvement over time.

Since 2014, the Connected Curriculum dimensions, their underpinning values and the creative possibilities afforded by re-thinking traditional and current practices have been discussed and responded to in various ways by faculty members, professional staff, students and alumni. Many actions have ensued:

- Establishing the Connected Curriculum Steering Committee, supported by a Development Group. Senior members of each academic Faculty and of key professional groups, along with student representatives, meet three times a year to oversee the initiative.
- Establishing Working Groups (currently ten), which report to the Steering Group. These focus on themes ranging from assessment and feedback, developing a connected learning environment, connecting postgraduates and enhancing workplace learning.
- Seconding academics and professional staff from across the institution to work on the initiative for a year, typically for one day a week, as Connected Curriculum Fellows.

- Funding more than 100 development projects focused on enhancing curriculum in line with one or more of the dimensions.
- Holding annual Teaching and Learning Conferences, at which both staff and students present on developments relating to the Connected Curriculum principles.
- Working with Academic Services to build references to the values and principles into the quality review cycles, for example by asking departments to reflect on their related developments in the self-evaluation document used for internal quality review panels.

3 Blossoming institutional initiatives

Along with the many examples of good practice identified and being developed within UCL's departments, a number of institution-wide initiatives have been instigated or significantly influenced by the Connected Curriculum framing. Some of these are outlined here.

Students as change makers

One very promising development has been the introduction of a scheme – UCL ChangeMakers (UCL 2016h) – designed to empower and resource students to take a lead in effecting change. Dr Jenny Marie, who leads the initiative, describes its purpose as 'to further UCL's aim of students being full partners in the university's future'. She explains that the original idea was to enable students to develop and carry out their own educational development 'change projects', by providing funding and central support for student-initiated projects. All the projects enhance the student learning experience but they vary widely. For example, one project has developed a series of videos on 3D printing, while another has organised Skype calls with a South American university to allow students to practise their language skills. Not all projects are discipline specific; students came from a variety of disciplines, for example, to consider how to enhance the module choice process.

In keeping with the core principle of the Connected Curriculum, the projects involve an element of enquiry – either by investigating the demand for a change, how it is best implemented or by evaluating a pilot. Students are offered training on research ethics, research methods, project management and leadership. As well as being supported centrally, students need to work with a member of UCL staff, who provides disciplinary support for the project, ensuring its relevance and utility for the context in which it will be implemented. As such, students learn through enquiry, connect with staff and have to produce outputs, such as reports, to persuade their audience of the utility of the change. The students are also all encouraged to discuss their work at UCL's annual Teaching and Learning conference.

Developing staff engagement and expertise

An important contributor to the success of the Connected Curriculum initiative is a cross-institutional developmental scheme that promotes a sense of community and connection among those who teach and/or support students: UCL Arena (UCL 2016i). Offering a series of developmental events, including Exchange Seminars in which any member of the institution can share approaches to practice and related education-focused scholarship, the scheme can also lead to professional recognition awards (Fellowships in four categories) aligned with the UK Professional Standards Framework. These awards contribute not only to individuals' academic and professional development but also to their claims for promotion to more senior grades.

More than 3,000 people have participated in activities in the first three years of the scheme, with more than 400 gaining Fellowship awards. In addition, more than a hundred colleagues from across the institution have become mentors and/or assessors for the fellowship scheme, sharing their own ideas and experiences of teaching with colleagues from across the eleven Faculties. UCL Arena thus provides many opportunities for dialogue and collaboration, including events that focus specifically on the dimensions of the Connected Curriculum framework.

Liberating the curriculum

Liberating the Curriculum is the name given to a working group which promotes the values and practices of 'liberating' the curriculum: that is, to reviewing programmes of study in the light of critiques that show that traditionally courses have been Eurocentric and male dominated. The Liberating the Curriculum working group, overseen by the Connected Curriculum Steering Group, comprises students as well as academic and professional staff. It aims to 'challenge traditional Eurocentric, male dominated curricula and to ensure the work of marginalised scholars on race, sexuality, gender and disability are fairly represented in curricula' (UCL 2016g).

The group has established an active online forum for discussing related issues and practices, run 'mythbusting' events, and developed a range of resources; these are made available on the virtual learning environment. It has also funded a series of projects on work to diversify the curriculum (work on race, gender, sexuality and disability) and produced a range of related videos. Six videos have been produced in which black and minority ethnic alumni describe their experiences of studying at UCL and the career paths they took, as well as an animation explaining the aims of the Liberating the Curriculum initiative. These activities are taking forward the Connected Curriculum principles of enabling diverse students to connect more effectively with one another and with alumni, challenging current practices that marginalise certain groups.

Developing a Connected Learning Environment

The kind of networked, research-based and interdisciplinary approach to education in the Connected Curriculum requires students to connect with each other, with staff, with research and with the outside world. These forms of connection require additional communication, collaboration and productivity tools, beyond those currently provided in the institution's virtual learning environment. A Digital Infrastructure working group has therefore been established to oversee the design, development and implementation of a new Connected Learning Environment, which is being taken forward through a capital project.

The Director of UCL Digital Education, Fiona Strawbridge, explains its focus:

> The working group involves students and staff with educational and technological expertise and meets termly. It has overseen scoping, requirements gathering, specification and the start of a procurement exercise, and will be involved in piloting and evaluating the new environment.

The aim is to provide an accessible, exciting and effective online learning environment that will help to cultivate the interdisciplinary and student-to-student connections captured in the Connected Curriculum dimensions.

R=T (Research equals Teaching)

The final example of an institution-wide initiative stemming from the Connected Curriculum is a scheme called R=T, run by Dr Vincent Tong, Dr Alex Standen and Dr Mina Sotiriou (UCL 2016j). This included a series of masterclasses led by distinguished senior academics, all passionately committed both to research and to student education, from the UCL community and beyond. Students from the UCL ChangeMakers scheme and postgraduate teaching assistants played an active part in the seminars, exploring innovative ideas with the academics. A number of related focus groups and events followed.

Inspired by the events and masterclasses, the R=T students worked with their partner professors and wrote sixteen chapters on research-based education; they are now planning to publish their 'outputs' in an edited book (Tong, Standen and Sotiriou, forthcoming), to highlight student perspectives on aspects of research-based education and advise academics on how to work with students to develop research-based approaches.

4 Challenges and opportunities

Challenges

While many creative ideas and promising activities have stemmed from introducing the Connected Curriculum at UCL, there have also been challenges. These include:

- **Devising a comprehensive communications strategy.** Introducing a multi-faceted way of framing educational discussions and developments to all of the varied participants in a large, dispersed institution comprising multiple research and learning communities is a big challenge. Patience, planning and resources are needed.
- **Communicating the 'liberating' ethos of the initiative.** An understandable, instinctive response by some faculty members to any institutionally agreed strategy is to imagine that it must be designed to control and to monitor practice, such is the sensitivity in academia to inappropriate 'managerialism' and the so-called audit culture. To convey the idea that the framework is designed to open up ideas and practices, not close them down, inevitably takes time and a shared willingness to take an open-minded, scholarly approach to analysing the opportunities afforded by it.
- **Communicating the framework's sensitivity to different disciplinary cultures.** In a similar vein, it takes time for members of some disciplinary communities to see the relevance of an initiative to their context. For some disciplines, it has been immediately appreciated and understood; for others, especially those for whom

the language of education and education development feels alien, more time is needed to realise its potential.

- **Connecting with students and their representatives.** Ensuring that dialogue is sustained between the institution and student representatives is yet another communications-related challenge. Working with the Student Union, UCLU, by, for example getting involved with its own Education Conference and by speaking with its sabbatical officers and student representatives about the initiative, has been very helpful here.
- **Recognising these enhancement activities within academic quality review and planning cycles.** The institution has an established quality review and planning cycle; it has been important to review this and create a more joined up cycle that enables departments to show holistically how they are taking action to enhance their curriculum.

Opportunities

Along with the challenges have come some very promising and sometimes unexpected developments. These include the development of new networks of people interested in taking forward a particular topic, who otherwise would not meet. This has the benefit of starting to break down some of the old divisions between academic and professional staff members, and between students and staff. Similarly, some very exciting connections have been made across disciplines and the initiative has been a vehicle for promoting more widely some exciting activities that were already underway, including the established UCL Global Citizenship programme (UCL 2016n) and the institution's innovative Object-Based Learning provision (UCL 2016o). During the development of the Connected Curriculum, UCL also merged with the world-renowned Institute of Education, which is affording many more opportunities for developmental and research collaborations.

At policy level, the institution has completely reviewed its promotions criteria, to reflect more accurately the value placed on student education and on the work of creating research-based learning opportunities for students. The Connected Curriculum initiative is also used to demonstrate commitment to educational excellence to external bodies, for example as part of the Teaching Excellence Framework cycle.

There has been much interest in the initiative externally, and scores of talks and keynote speeches on the Connected Curriculum concept have been given at institutions and conferences across the UK and Europe. This makes a demand on staff time but the benefits of such a high level of external networking for the sharing of good practice are very high. In a related vein, opportunities for researching change, both at UCL and in other institutions also undertaking curriculum change programmes, are now considerable. We are currently researching institutional change under the heading 'Curriculum as institutional story', and welcome contact with higher education institutions anywhere in the world that might be interested in collaborating with us in this kind of research.

5 Looking ahead

UCL aims to empower departments to be bolder and braver in their choices as they forge new connections between their research and student education, and not to feel that they must conform to traditional patterns of teaching. It recognises that this is not easy and that if institutional systems – for example, student record systems, virtual learning environments, regulations or timetabling – block changes to promising educational developments identified by departments, that these systems need to be reviewed. The intention is to direct institutional resources to the places where they are most needed and where they can result in the best possible student education. This is, and needs to be, part of a long-term plan, as outlined in the twenty-year UCL 2034 strategy.

The intention for the Connected Curriculum initiative is thus both simple and far reaching: to act as a catalyst for enabling faculty, professional staff and students alike to take a step back and ask some fundamental, values-based questions about what a university is, and about what kinds of educational developments they want to prioritise, within and across disciplines, in the years ahead. The accounts that departments and cross-departmental networks are able to give of their own creative developments, and the stories of the diverse students who benefit from them, will be our means of evaluating its success.

0
Moving forward

There is no golden city that is 'beyond the divide'.
What is important is the journey we take;
the processes of putting into practice the values
and aspirations of an inclusive, scholarly
higher education community.

Angela Brew (2006, 180)

Reviewing programmes by using the Connected Curriculum framework

This monograph has offered a curriculum framework in the spirit of opening up productive, shared conversations about values and practices. These conversations will ideally cut across departmental and disciplinary divisions, helping to build even better academic, personal and professional connections between the diverse members of the higher education community.

One way of starting the conversation is for departments and programme teams to discuss their current practices using twenty preliminary questions as a catalyst (Table 10.1). These questions, linked to the core principle and six dimensions of the Connected Curriculum framework, will ideally be considered not only by academics and professional staff but also by students and, where possible, alumni.

A second way of summarising the issues raised by the framework is to imagine how alumni of a connected programme might reflect on their experience, in contrast with alumni reflecting on a disconnected programme. Two imagined and contrasting students' recollections of their experience illustrate the two extremes.

Table 10. 1 The Connected Curriculum in 20 Questions

Dimensions	Key questions for departments and programme teams
Core principle (Ch.2) **Students learn through research and enquiry**	1. Are students encountering specific questions addressed by researchers and learning to articulate their own research questions, at every level of study? 2. Can we adjust our teaching methods, student assessments and other aspects of departmental practice to prioritise engaging all students actively in research and critical enquiry?
Dimension 1 (Ch.3) **Students connect with researchers and with the institution's research**	3. Do students have regular opportunities to learn about the institution's research and other current research relevant to their studies? 4. Are students meeting with researchers and engaging with their work, for example through group activities such as 'Meet the Researcher'? 5. Are students exploring the intellectual, policy-related, practical and ethical challenges associated with current research, and recognising their relevance to professional life more widely?
Dimension 2 (Ch.4) **A throughline of research activity is built into each programme**	6. Is there a well designed core sequence of modules, units and/or learning activities through which students steadily build their research skills and understandings, and is this explicit to students? 7. Are students explicitly challenged to make intellectual connections between different elements of their programme? 8. Can students have some flexibility and even take risks with their research-related activities, for example by working towards a Showcase Portfolio for which they can curate their best work?
Dimension 3 (Ch.5) **Students make connections across disciplines and out to the world**	9. Is the programme of study structured so that students need to step outside their home discipline(s) and see through at least one other disciplinary lens? 10. Are students required to make explicit connections between disciplinary perspectives, for example by collaborating with students of other disciplines to analyse evidence and issues? 11. Through making interdisciplinary connections, are students challenged to

Dimension 4 (Ch.6)

Students connect academic learning with workplace learning

12. Are all students on the programme(s) able to analyse the ways in which their academic learning is relevant to the world of work?

13. Do students have explicit opportunities to prepare for the workplace, for example through meeting alumni, shadowing and work placements and, where appropriate, through critiquing the notions of work and professionalism in society?

14. Can students articulate effectively the skills and knowledge they have developed through their research-related activities and through their wider studies and experiences, and showcase these to future employers?

Dimension 5 (Ch.7)

Students learn to produce outputs – assessments directed at an audience

15. Are some student assessments outward-facing, directed at an audience, thereby enabling them to connect with local and/or wider communities (whether online or face-to-face)?

16. Are student assessments across the programme suitably varied, enabling them to develop a range of skills including expertise in digital practices and communications?

17. Are students required to revisit and use feedback on their tasks, both formative and summative, in order to improve their work?

Dimension 6 (Ch.8)

Students connect with each other, across phases and with alumni

18. Do students have frequent opportunities to meet and participate in collaborative enquiry with one another in diverse groups?

19. Are they building connections with students in other year groups, for example through events or mentoring schemes?

20. Can students meet and learn from diverse alumni and build a strong sense of belonging to an inclusive research and learning community?

Student A

I arrived at university and was told about the bank of modules I could choose from to get my degree. There were quite a few options and I wasn't always sure how they connected or why sometimes they overlapped and the tutors didn't seem to realise this. For most modules I took, I was given fairly specific guidance about the resources I should access. At other times I was supposed to investigate for myself without really knowing whether I was going about it the right way. I rarely heard anything about the lecturers' own research or about recent research in general.

I focused on completing the assessments for each separate module; they were all either written assignments or exams. Once I'd completed a module, I didn't think much about what I'd learned from it. Because I was always with a different student group, I got to know very few of my fellow students and I rarely had the opportunity to work with them directly. And I didn't get much opportunity to discuss how the different aspects of the degree related to one another. When I was interviewed for a job after I'd graduated, they asked me what skills I'd developed on my course and what I could offer a large, diverse organisation and I wasn't able to give a very convincing answer.

Looking back, I didn't seem to have much chance to investigate ideas for myself – I could have done, because there's so much available online now and I have plenty of ideas of my own. I passed all my exams and ended up with a degree, so it should help me in the future, but at the time I didn't think much about how I might use my new knowledge out in the world or how it relates to any of the big global challenges we all seem to be faced with today. It was good but seemed quite narrow. I think I could have been more personally engaged, and more intellectually stimulated, if I had been able to get involved more actively with the life and work of the department.

Student B

We arrived at university and the programme leader and lecturers explained that the journey through my degree had been carefully designed. There would be opportunities for us to choose different modules during each year of study but, at every level, there would also be at least one Connections module where we would have guided conversations with an academic tutor about our developing perspectives on the subject.

The primary way of learning in our modules was through active enquiry, which meant there was a focus on thinking about complex questions and how to answer them – how to look at them from different perspectives. We regularly heard about the latest research in the field and had opportunities to question our tutors, many of whom were researchers themselves. The tutors were all experts – if they were not currently researching, they were up to date with the latest research and some were particularly knowledgeable about education, which helped to make the teaching and the whole programme really engaging.

We were able to collaborate on some group projects with our fellow students and we investigated how groups work, evaluating our own roles and contributions. There were even opportunities for us to be mentored by students in the years above and also to meet alumni and hear about how they are now using their degrees.

We were encouraged to access educational materials from a wide variety of sources and used these to help us question the ideas we were learning about. We began to learn about how different knowledge traditions are created in our complicated and diverse world, and how some voices and perspectives have been marginalised.

A connected set of opportunities for us to investigate ran through the centre of the degree programme. This happened primarily through the sequence of Connections modules, which enabled us to build an online Showcase Portfolio of our investigative work. I have been able to access my portfolio since graduating and to make it available to various people, including my current employer. While producing our work, we were given plenty of freedom to access resources from beyond the university to enrich our understandings of the key topics.

Not everything I did would eventually count towards my final marks so I could try things out, even take some risks. At each level of study, alongside a Connections module, I took modules with a range of different kinds of assessments, which challenged me to develop different ways of thinking. But we were all explicitly encouraged, by lecturers and by our academic tutor, to make links across all of the different topic areas covered in the degree.

(Continued)

Through the Connections modules we were also encouraged to develop our own specific areas of interest and follow them up, using our initiative and imagination. Sometimes I worked collaboratively with a group of my fellow students; at other times I worked independently. I learned some very useful things about working in groups and included this in my Showcase Portfolio.

In my final year, I completed a substantial independent research project, which formed the final part of my Portfolio and really showcases what I can do. I presented my work-in-progress to first-year students and alumni at an undergraduate research conference and also enjoyed hearing postgraduate students present their research through the departments' research seminar series. That was a good way of getting to know other people.

By the time I graduated, I was confident that I could describe and apply my current knowledge and skills really well. But more than that, I could express confidence in my ability to investigate anything, anywhere, and to make sound judgments about my findings. I could also present those findings in a variety of formats. Because of my active learning, the intellectual choices I'd made and the opportunities I'd taken to work with others and present my ideas to different audiences, I feel empowered as a graduate to contribute to the workplace and to society, and to speak out with confidence about my knowledge, skills, views and values.

Like the 'twenty questions' above, the two students' narratives can provoke discussion in departments. They are stylised accounts, of course, and different disciplinary contexts will make certain elements of practice more appealing and more practical to some programme teams than others. The intention is to stimulate dialogue and creative thinking about how the curriculum might move forward in coming years. What kind of story would you like your graduates to tell of *their* experiences? And what kind of story would your students like to tell about themselves?

2 A question of values

Reviewing curriculum raises important underlying questions for institutions and departments. How inclusive is our community, and our decision-making, as we decide where we want to go? Do students have a voice? We need to ask ourselves whether professional and administrative colleagues, with their vital areas of expertise, have an equal seat at the table and whether junior faculty members engage fully in the debate. Particular attention needs to be paid to whether women, black and minority ethnic colleagues, colleagues with disabilities and others who are not well represented in university leadership teams are empowered to become full and equal participants in our learning and research communities.

Institutional and departmental values need to be explicitly discussed. There is no such thing as values-free education, or values-free research: all activities in these fields are value-laden, whether explicitly or tacitly. Values are inherent, for example, in what is selected as a valid topic for research, in how research studies are funded, constructed and communicated, and in who conducts and benefits from the research. They are profoundly implicated in what is taught as the 'canon' in a given discipline and in the silences of the curriculum: the areas of focus and kinds of knowledge that are excluded. Values are also evident in *how* programmes are taught. We need to consider the relationships and power dynamics between teachers and students, between researchers and teachers, and between scholars, students, professionals and the community. Who are the gatekeepers? Who contributes to decision-making? These themes will ideally infuse discussions about possibilities for curriculum and institutional development.

3 Challenges for departments and institutions

The task of engaging students even more meaningfully with research within and across disciplines, and of enabling them to connect purposefully with one another, should not be underestimated (Locke 2005). Departments, like students, need the right balance between freedom and mission if they are to enhance their curriculum. But institutions need to provide an environment in which this balance is possible: current institutional and even national policies may even need to be revised.

A number of issues have to be taken into consideration if creating these new connections is to be mutually beneficial:

1. Providing academic guidance and support for diverse students

Engaging students more fully in research and active enquiry focuses attention on support structures. Taking an active role in this way is more demanding for students than simply passively receiving knowledge and reproducing it in an examination. In an internationalised higher education sector, students bring very diverse prior experiences and expectations. They may be challenged particularly in five areas: information literacy; personal beliefs about learning and knowledge; personal self-confidence; enquiry framing and direction setting; and peer collaboration (Levy and Petrulis 2012). This means that institutions need to resource the provision of structured student guidance by academics and related professional staff. Investment may well be needed in areas such as academic tutoring, libraries and resource centres, online support networks and mentoring schemes.

2. Supporting researchers

Connecting students with researchers should not add an inappropriate burden to the lives of the researchers whose work is so vitally important. Researchers have very demanding roles and are typically very committed to their work; they can also be overstretched by having to juggle the demands of research itself with those of negotiating time-bound contracts, submitting grant applications, engaging in peer review and building up their own publications profile. Researchers can benefit greatly from becoming engaged with student education, particularly when students are learning through research and active enquiry. However, they need to be supported, developed and rewarded for doing so.

3. Institutional structures and regulations

The challenges of connecting research with education may be further complicated by institutional structures and academic regulations. Universities and their sub-divisions may be structured in such a way that those leading on the research mission work separately from those leading on student education. Committee structures typically sustain this separation: where, in the committee structure, can sufficient attention be paid to building productive synergies between research and education? A steering group, for example, could be set up for that very purpose. Academic regulations, too, may need to be reviewed to enable students to benefit from research-based education. The regulations need to facilitate, rather than limit, the development of an engaging curriculum.

4. Roles, reward and recognition

The challenge for departments may be further complicated by systems of reward and recognition across the higher education sector

Unhelpful divisions between types of academic role in higher education need to be revisited. Roles vary across the sector internationally but, in many contexts, there is a historic bifurcation of roles: some university teachers are also researchers, while others undertake education-focused roles. Both make a vital contribution to the ecology of a research-rich curriculum but issues of inequality arise. For example, in research-intensive institutions in the UK, a significant majority of those in traditional academic researcher-educator roles are men, whereas the majority in education-focused roles are women (Fung and Gordon 2016). Yet the markers of prestige and opportunities for progression are more favourable in the male-dominated group. This kind of systemic imbalance is contributed to in some higher education institutions by employing large numbers of people on short-term, temporary contracts (Locke and Bennion 2010), which can be destabilising and demotivating for both employees and students. A divided, discouraged workforce will certainly be a barrier to the aims and values of the Connected Curriculum: surely a better way is to build more stability of employment along with greater permeability between types of role, so that everyone can play to their scholarly strengths whether these are as educators, researchers or both (Fung 2016; Fung and Gordon 2016). Technical specialists and professionals undertaking a wide range of roles also need to be included fully in curriculum development and rewarded appropriately: they contribute richly, in various contexts, to students' learning.

5. Developing partnerships with students

As noted earlier, it is vital that students play an active part in taking forward new developments. Schemes that enable them to take leadership roles and work in partnership with universities are proliferating (Healey 2016) and they show how active and creative students can be if they are included fully in decision-making processes, the setting of goals and the articulation of values. Token inclusion of student representatives on committees is no longer enough: students need a real voice and to become partners in reality not just in name.

6. Forging links with local and wider communities

A number of elements of the Connected Curriculum approach rely on building strong connections between students' programmes of study and wider society. Many people would agree that this is a good idea in principle but it takes time and focused expertise to do this well. Institutions need to invest in human resource, preferably dedicated posts, whose focus is on this task; this is particularly important where there are large student numbers. A specialist role may be needed to forge connections with community members (including alumni) as developmental partners, creating links with organisations and industry in order to promote opportunities for students to engage with the workplace through shadowing or internships, and helping faculty members and students to find audiences and partners for the outward-facing work they produce.

7. Developing physical and virtual learning environments suited to research-based education.

Some current teaching and learning spaces are unsuited to research-based education. Flexible physical environments are needed in which students can meet and collaborate both during and between formally taught sessions. Online spaces that promote connections between different groups of students and between students and academics, including researchers, also need to be developed. For example, where virtual learning environments are designed on a module-by-module basis, they may need to be reviewed and/or enhanced; the virtual environment needs to make it easy, not difficult, to collaborate across modular and disciplinary boundaries.

8. Resourcing development of, and research into, higher education

Finally, the higher education sector as a whole needs to invest in research *into* its own practices, with a focus on building better synergies between its complementary missions. Such research can be set within a values-based commitment to ensuring that the sector makes the strongest possible contribution to the common good, both locally and globally (Marginson 2016), building on and connecting the existing related expertise located in a wide range of relevant university disciplines. If we are to commit to research-based education, changes made to curriculum need to be theoretically strong and evidence-informed. Similarly, resources need to be invested in those who provide specialist expertise in education for departments, including those who are expert in learning technologies.

These are among the issues that need to be addressed if students are to benefit fully from studying in a research-rich environment. Goals that suit a particular discipline need to be realistic; a long-term plan for change is needed because quick solutions are unlikely to be effective. Time needs to be made available to all involved with planning for change.

To sum up, the onus on developing a research-based curriculum, whereby students and communities benefit even more fully from the research that takes place in higher education, cannot just be on individual faculty members and their professional colleagues, who already undertake very busy, demanding and multi-faceted roles. Institutional leaders, structures, policies and funding practices need to support the mission.

4 Conclusions: looking to the future

The co-location of education and research in universities is a great strength. Research shows students and all scholars where the edges of knowledge are, as well as what is known. This has always been important but it is absolutely vital in this politically volatile era of 'alternative facts' and 'fake news'. Connecting with research enables us all to see how gaps in knowledge are tackled, how new knowledge is created and how it can be effectively communicated with diverse audiences. Engagement by the higher education sector with society, already strong, has the potential to become even stronger if all students are empowered to participate actively in research and enquiry, especially if they can engage local and wider communities with their findings. Each university can, as Barnett puts it, become 'aware of its interconnectedness with society and [put] its resources towards the development of societal and personal well-being' (Barnett 2011, 453). Barnett writes:

> What is surely clear is that the university has to accept its own responsibility to think seriously about the matter: just what is it to be a university in the 21st century? (Barnett 2011, 454)

The Connected Curriculum initiative aims to cultivate new ways of thinking and speaking about what it is to be a university, by encouraging disciplines to build on their own distinctiveness and the special characteristics of research in the field. It provides an illustrative menu of practices and these will certainly vary in applicability, depending on context. However, there is a consistent feature, a watermark: the philosophical commitment to critical enquiry informed by dialogue, to fostering dispositions for testing what we think we know and to extending our knowledge horizons by connecting with those of others. Equally important is the values-based commitment to the public good; research and enquiry are about 'acquiring, validating and using knowledge', but they also aim to 'address fundamental issues of the creation and control of knowledge' (UNESCO 2015, 79).

The position taken here, then, is that higher education curriculum is not just for the benefit of individual students, enabling them to succeed personally in a competitive, economy-driven world but for the benefit of wider society. Connecting education more readily with research can enable students to work in partnership with universities to develop even stronger societal and global missions. Breaking down longstanding divisions between research and education can also build stronger bridges between research, education, professional practice and society. As these boundaries are crossed, so older hierarchical distinctions become less powerful, and new kinds of conversations and collaborations become possible.

The Connected Curriculum framing has already opened up many collaborative conversations about new possibilities for higher education. It has also helped to cultivate developments in practice, both within its home institution and across wider national and international settings. If it continues to do so, and both students and communities benefit, it will have fulfilled its intentions.

:erlind, Gerlese S. 2008. 'An Academic Perspective on Research and Being a Researcher: An Integration of the Literature.' *Studies in Higher Education* 33 1:17-31. doi: 10.1080/03075070701794775

*ple, M. W. 2005. 'Education, Markets, and an Audit Culture.' *Critical Quarterly* 47:11-29. doi:10.1111/j.0011-1562.2005.00611.x.

thurs, Leilani and Alexis Templeton. 2009. 'Coupled Collaborative In-class Activities and Individual Follow-up Homework Promote Interactive Engagement and Improve Student Learning Outcomes in a College-level Environmental Geology Course (Geological Sciences, CU).' *Journal of Geoscience Education* 57 5:356-371.

ins, Sunny, John E. Mitchell, Abel Nyamapfene and Emanuela Tilley. 2015. 'Work in Progress: Multi-disciplinary Curriculum Review of Engineering Education. UCL's Integrated Engineering Programme,' IEEE Global Engineering Education Conference (EDUCON), Tallinn 2015. 844-846. doi: 10.1109/EDUCON.2015.7096070

rnett, Ronald. 2000. 'Supercomplexity and the Curriculum.' *Studies in Higher Education* 25 3:255-265. doi: 10.1080/713696156

rnett, Ronald. 2011. 'The Coming of the Ecological University.' *Oxford Review of Education* 37 4:439-455. doi: 10.1080/03054985.2011.595550

:nett, Ronald. 2016. *Understanding the University: Institution, Idea, Possibilities.* Abingdon and New York: Routledge.

:nett, Ronald and Kelly Coate. 2005. *Engaging the Curriculum in Higher Education.* Buckingham: SRHE and Open University Press.

:ter-Magolda, M. 2004. 'Self-authorship as the common goal of 21st century education.' In *Learning partnerships: Theory and Models of Practice to Educate for Self-Authorship.*

:her, Tony. 1989. *Academic Tribes and Territories.* Buckingham: Open University Press.

:her, Tony and Paul R. Trowler 2001. 2nd edition: 1st edition 1989. *Academic Tribes and Territories: Intellectual Enquiry and the Culture of the Disciplines.* Buckingham and Philadelphia: The Society for Research into Higher Education and Open University Press.

idermacher, G.W.G., M.G.A. oude Egbrink, I.H.A.P Wolfhagen and D. H. J. M. Dolmans. 2016. 'Unravelling Quality Culture in Higher Education: a Realist Review.' *Higher Education* doi:10.1007/s10734-015-9979-2

sta, Gert. 2006. *Beyond Learning: Democratic Education.* Colarado: Paradigm.

gs, John. 2003. *Teaching for Quality Learning at University.* 2nd edition. Maidenhead: Open University Press.

/Johnson, Jo. 2015. 'Teaching at the Heart of the System.' Speech to Universities UK, 1 July 2015. Department for Business, Innovation and Skills. https://www.gov.uk/government/speeches/teaching-at-the-heart-of-the-system

:kmore, Paul and Camille B. Kandiko. 2012. *Strategic Curriculum Change in Universities: Global Trends.* Abingdon: Routledge.

:kmore, Paul, Richard Blackwell and Martin Edmondsen. 2016. *Tackling Wicked Issues: Prestige and Employment Outcomes in the Teaching Excellence Framework.* HEPI Occasional Paper 14. http://www.hepi.ac.uk/wp-content/uploads/2016/09/Hepi_TTWI-Web.pdf

:kmore, Paul, Zoe H. Bulaitis, Anna H. Jackman and Emrullah Tan. 2016. 'Employability in Higher Education: A Review of Practice and Strategies around the World.' Report commissioned by Pearson Efficacy and Research. https://uk.pearson.com/content/dam/region-core/uk/pearson-uk/documents/about/news-and-policy/employability-models-synthesis.pdf

Blessinger, Patrick and John M. Carfora. eds. 2014. *Inquiry-Based Learning for the Arts, Humanities and Social Sciences: A Conceptual and Practical Resource for Educators: 2.* Innovations in Higher Education Teaching and Learning. Bingley, UK: Emerald.

Bloxham, Sue. 2009. 'Marking and Moderation in the UK: False Assumptions and Wasted Resources.' *Assessment and Evaluation in Higher Education* 34 2:209–220.

Bloxham, Sue and Pete Boyd. 2007. *Developing Effective Assessment in Higher Education: A Practical Guide.* Maidenhead: Open University Press. https://www.mheducation.co.uk/openup/chapters/9780335221073.pdf

Boden, Rebecca and Maria Nedeva. 2010. Employing Discourse: Universities and Graduate 'Employability'. *Journal of Education Policy* 25 1:37–54. doi;10.1080/02680930903349489

Boix Mansilla, Veronica and Flossie Chua. 2016. 'Signature Pedagogies in Global Competence Education: Understanding Quality Teaching Practice'. Interdisciplinary and Global Studies – Internal Working Paper, Project Zero: Harvard Graduate School of Education. http://schd.ws/hosted_files/wissit2016/e1/VBM%20paper%20on%20Sign%20Ped.pdf

Boud, David and Nancy Falchikov. eds. 2007. *Rethinking Assessment in Higher Education: Learning for the longer term.* Abingdon, Oxford: Routledge.

Boud, David and Nicky Solomon. eds. 2001. *Work-based Learning: A New Higher Education?* Buckingham, UK: SRHE and Open University Press.

Boyer, Ernest L. 1990. *Scholarship Reconsidered: Priorities of the Professoriate.* Princeton, NJ: Carnegie Foundation for the Advancement of Teaching.

Boyer, Ernest L. 1996. 'The Scholarship of Engagement.' *Journal of Public Service and Outreach* 1 1:11–20.

Boyer Commission on Educating Undergraduates in the Research University. 1998. *Reinventing Undergraduate Education: A Blueprint for America's Research Universities.* https://www.adelaide.edu.au/rsd/evidence/related-articles/Boyer_Report.pdf

Boyer Commission on Educating Undergraduates in the Research University. 2001. *Reinventing Undergraduate Education: Three Years After the Boyer Report.* Accessed 09 October 2016. https://dspace.sunyconnect.suny.edu/handle/1951/26013

Brew, Angela. 2001. 'Conceptions of Research: A phenomenographic study.' *Studies in Higher Education* 26 3:271–285.

Brew, Angela. 2006. *Research and Teaching: Beyond the Divide.* London: Palgrave Macmillan.

Brew, Angela. 2012. 'Teaching and Research: New Relationships and their Implications for Inquiry-based Teaching and Learning in Higher Education.' *Higher Education Research & Development* 311:101–114. doi: 10.1080/07294360.2012.642844

British Academy. 2016. *Crossing Paths: Interdisciplinary Institutions, Careers, Education and Applications.* http://www.britac.ac.uk/sites/default/files/Crossing%20Paths%20-%20Full%20Report.pdf

Bruffee, Kenneth. 1999. *Collaborative Learning: Higher Education, Interdependence, and the Authority of Knowledge.* 2nd edition. Baltimore: Johns Hopkins University Press.

Bruner, Jerome. 1986. *Actual Minds, Possible Worlds.* Cambridge MA and London: Harvard University Press.

Bruner, Jerome. 2002. *Making Stories: Law, Literature, Life.* New York: Farrar, Straus and Giroux.

Bryan, Cordelia and Karen Clegg. eds. 2006. *Innovative Assessment in Higher Education.* Abingdon: Routledge.

Caple, Helen and Mike Bogle. 2013. 'Making Group Assessment Transparent: What Wikis can Contribute to Collaborative Projects.' *Assessment & Evaluation in Higher Education* 38 2:198–210. doi: 10.1080/02602938.2011.618879

Carnell, Brent. 2016. 'Aiming for Autonomy: Formative Peer Assessment in a Final-year Undergraduate Course.' *Assessment & Evaluation in Higher Education* 4 1 8:1269–1283 doi: 10.1080/02602938.2015.1077196

Chatterjee, Helen J. and Leonie Hannan. 2015. *Engaging the Senses: Object-Based Learning in Higher Education.* Farnham, UK and Burlington, USA: Ashgate Publishing Ltd.

Clarke, Jillian L. and David Boud. 2016. 'Refocusing Portfolio Assessment: Curating for Feedback and Portrayal.' *Innovations in Education and Teaching International.* doi: 10.1080/14703297.2016.1250664

Clandinin, Jean. 2000. *Narrative Inquiry: Experience and Story in Qualitative Research.* San Francisco: Jossey-Bass.

Clifford, V. A. 2009. 'Engaging the Disciplines in Internationalising the Curriculum.' *International Journal for Academic Development* 14 2:133–143.

Clough, P. 2002. *Narratives and Fictions in Educational Research*. Buckingham: Open University Press.

Cole, Doug and Maureen Tibby. 2013. *Defining and Developing your Approach to Employability: A Framework for Higher Education Institutions*. York: Higher Education Academy https://www.heacademy.ac.uk/system/files/resources/employability_framework.pdf

Collini, Stefan. 2012. *What Are Universities For?* London and New York: Penguin.

Coughlan, Tony and Leigh-Anne Perryman. 2011. Something for Everyone? The Different Approaches of Academic Disciplines to Open Educational Resources and the Effect on Widening Participation. *Journal of Open, Flexible and Distance Learning* 15 2:11–27.

CURQ (Council on Undergraduate Research Quarterly). 2016. Home page. http://www.cur.org/publications/spring_2012_curq_on_the_web/

Deem, Rosemary, Sam Hillyard and Mike Reed. 2007. *Knowledge, Higher Education and the New Managerialism*. Oxford: Oxford University Press.

Delors, Jacques/UNESCO. 1996. 'Learning, the Treasure Within: International Commission on Education for the Twenty-first Century.' Report to UNESCO by the International Commission on Education for the Twenty-first Century. Paris: UNESCO Publishing. http://unesdoc.unesco.org/images/0010/001095/109590eo.pdf

Dezure, Deborah, Lisa R. Lattuca, Kathryn Dey Huggett, Nora C. Smith and Clifton F. Conrad. 2002. *Encyclopedia of Education*. http://www.encyclopedia.com/doc/1G2-3403200167.html

Dohaney, Jacqueline, Erik Brogt and Ben Kennedy. 2012. 'Successful Curriculum Development and Evaluation of Group Work in an Introductory Mineralogy Laboratory (Earth and Ocean Sciences, UBC).' *Journal of Geoscience Education* 60:21–33.

Dwyer, Claire. 2001. Linking Research and Teaching: A Staff-Student Interview Project. *Journal of Geography in Higher Education*, 25 3:357–366. doi: 10.1080/03098260120067646

Elken, Mari and Sabine Wollscheid. 2016. 'The Relationship between Research and Education: Typologies and Indicators: A Literature Review.' Oslo, Norway: Nordic Institute for Studies in Innovation, Research and Education (NIFU).

Erben, Michael. 2000. 'Ethics, Education, Narrative Communication and Biography.' *Educational Studies* 26 3:379–390. doi:10.1080/03055690050137178

European Commission/EACEA/Eurydice. 2015. 'The European Higher Education Area in 2015: Bologna Process Implementation Report.' Luxembourg: Publications Office of the European Union. http://eacea.ec.europa.eu/education/eurydice/documents/thematic_reports/182EN.pdf

European Union. 2014. 'The Erasmus Impact Study: Effects of Mobility on the Skills and Employability of Students and the Internationalisation of Higher Education Institutions.' http://ec.europa.eu/dgs/education_culture/repository/education/library/study/2014/erasmus-impact_en.pdf

EUA (European University Association). 2006. *Quality Culture in European Universities: A Bottom-up Approach*. Report on the three rounds of the quality culture project 2002–2006. EUA: Brussels. http://www.eua.be/eua/jsp/en/upload/Quality_Culture_2002_2003.1150459570109.pdf

Evans, Carol. 2013. 'Making Sense of Assessment Feedback in Higher Education.' *Review of Educational Research* 83 1:70–120. doi: 10.3102/0034654312474350

Evans, Carol, Daniel Muijs and Michael Tomlinson. 2015. *Engaged Student Learning: High-Impact Strategies to Enhance Student Achievement*. York, UK: Higher Education Academy. https://www.heacademy.ac.uk/sites/default/files/engaged_student_learning_high-impact_pedagogies.pdf

Fairfield, Paul. ed. 2012. *Education, Dialogue and Hermeneutics*. London: Continuum-3PL.

Falchikov, Nancy. 2007. 'The Place of Peers in Learning and Assessment,' in *Rethinking Assessment in Higher Education: Learning for the longer term*. Edited by D. Boud and N. Falchikov. 128–143. London: Routledge.

Fung, Dilly. 2007. *Telling Tales of Higher Education*. PhD Thesis. University of Exeter.

Fung, Dilly. 2016. 'Strength-based Scholarship and Good Education: The Scholarship Circle.' *Innovations in Education and Teaching International*. doi: 10.1080/14703297.2016.1257951

Fung, Dilly and Claire Gordon. 2016. 'Rewarding Educators and Education Leaders in Research-intensive Universities.' York: Higher Education Academy. https://www.heacademy.ac.uk/sites/default/files/rewarding_educators_and_education_leaders.pdf

Fung, D., J. Besters-Dilger and R. van der Vaart. 2017. 'Excellent Education in Research-rich Universities.' Position Paper: League of European Universities (LERU). http://www.leru. org/files/general/LERU%20Position%20Paper%20Excellent%20Education.pdf

Gadamer, Hans-Georg. 2004. *Truth and Method.* 2nd revised edition. Translated by J. W. Marshall. London: Continuum.

Geertz, Clifford. 1973. *The Interpretation of Cultures: Selected Essays.* New York: Basic Books.

Geertz, Clifford. 1982. 'The Way We Think Now: Toward an Ethnography of Modern Thought.' *Bulletin of the American Academy of Arts and Sciences* 35 5:14–34. http://links.jstor.org/ sici?sici=0002-712X%28198202%2935%3A5%3C14%3ATWWTNT%3E2.0.CO%3B2-Z

Georghiou, Luke. 2015. 'Value of Research.' Policy Paper by the Research, Innovation, and Science Policy Experts (RISE), European Commission. https://ec.europa.eu/research/ innovation-union/pdf/expert-groups/rise/georghiou-value_research.pdf

Habermas, Jürgen. 1996. 'What is Universal Pragmatics?' In Outhwaite ed. 1996. *The Habermas reader.* Cambridge: Polity Press 118–131.

Harland, Tony. 2016. 'Teaching to Enhance Research.' *Higher Education Research & Development.* 35 3:461–472.

Harland, Tony, Angela McLean, Rob Wass, Ellen Miller and Kwong Nui. 2015. 'An Assessment Arms Race and its Fallout: High-stakes Grading and the Case for Slow Scholarship.' *Assessment & Evaluation in Higher Education* 40 4:528–541. doi: 10.1080/02602938.2014.931927

Haslam, S. Alexander, Stephen D. Reicher and Michael J. Platow. 2011. *The New Psychology of Leadership: Identity, Influence and Power.* Hove and New York: Psychology Press.

Healey, Mick. 2016. 'Students as Partners and Change Agents: A Selected Bibliography.' www. mickhealey.co.uk/resources.

Healey, Mick and Alan Jenkins. 2009. 'Developing Undergraduate Research and Inquiry.' York: Higher Education Academy. http://www.heacademy.ac.uk/assets/York/documents/ resources/publications/DevelopingUndergraduate_Final.pdf

Higher Education Academy. 2016. 'Embedding employability.' https://www.heacademy.ac.uk/ enhancement/frameworks/framework-embedding-employability-higher-education

Hoon, Chng Huang and Peter Looker. 2013. 'On the margins of SoTL [Scholarship of Teaching and Learning] Discourse: An Asian Perspective.' *Teaching and Learning Inquiry* 1 1:131–145.

Horlacher, Renekka. 2015. *The Educated Subject and the German Concept of Bildung: A Comparative Cultural History.* Abingdon and New York: Routledge.

Hoskinson, Anne-Marie, M. Caballero and J. Knight. 2013. 'How Can We Improve Problem Solving in Undergraduate Biology? Applying Lessons from 30 Years of Physics Education Research.' *CBE-Life Sciences Education* 12 2:153–161.

Jacobs, J. A. 2013. *In Defense of Disciplines.* London: The University of Chicago Press.

Jaques, David. 2000. *Learning in groups: A Handbook for Improving Group Work.* 3rd edition. London and New York: RoutledgeFalmer.

Jenkins, Alan. 2004. *A Guide to the Research Evidence of Teaching-Research Relations.* York: Higher Education Academy.

Jessop, Tansy and Barbara Maleckar. 2016. 'The Influence of Disciplinary Assessment Patterns on Student Learning: A Comparative Study.' *Studies in Higher Education* 41 4:696–711. doi: 10.1080/03075079.2014.943170

Knight, Peter T. 2002. 'Summative Assessment in Higher Education: Practices in Disarray.' *Studies in Higher Education* 27 3:275–286.

Knight, Peter T. and Mantz Yorke. 2006a. 'Embedding Employability into the Curriculum.' The Higher Education Academy Learning and Employability Series. York: Higher Education Academy. http://www.qualityresearchinternational.com/esecttools/esect-pubs/yorkeknightembedding.pdf

Knight, Peter T. and Mantz Yorke. 2006b. 'Employability: Judging and Communicating Achievements.' York: Higher Education Academy. http://www.qualityresearchinterna-tional.com/esecttools/esectpubs/knightyorkeachievement.pdf

Kuhn, Thomas. 1970. *The Structure of Scientific Revolutions.* 2nd edition. Chicago and London: University of Chicago Press.

League of European Research Universities (LERU). 2016. 'Citizen Science at Universities: Trends, Guidelines and Recommendations.' Advice Paper No. 20 – October 2016. http://www.leru org/files/publications/LERU_AP20_citizen_science.pdf

Levy, Philippa and Robert Petrulis. 2012. 'How do First Year University Students Experience Inquiry and Research, and what are the Implications for the Practice o

Inquiry-based Learning?' *Studies in Higher Education* 37 1:85–101. http://dx.doi.org/10.1080/03075079.2010.499166

Locke, William. 2005. 'Integrating Research and Teaching Strategies: Implications for Institutional Management and Leadership in the United Kingdom.' *Higher Education Management and Policy* 16 3. doi: http://dx.doi.org/10.1787/hemp-v16-art25-en

Locke, W. and A. Bennion. 2010. 'The Changing Academic Profession in the UK and Beyond.' Universities UK Research Report. http://www.universitiesuk.ac.uk/highereducation/Documents/2010/TheChangingHEProfession.pdf

Lyall, Catherine, Laura Meagher, Justyna Bandola Gill and Ann Kettle. 2016. 'Interdisciplinary Provision in Higher Education.' https://www.heacademy.ac.uk/sites/default/files/interdisciplinary_provision_in_he.pdf

Marginson, Simon. 2008. 'Ideas of a University' for the Global Era. Keynote speech. The University of Hong Kong. http://citeseerx.ist.psu.edu/viewdoc/download?doi=10.1.1.662.1954 &rep=rep1&type=pdf

Marginson, Simon. 2016. *Higher Education and the Common Good.* Melbourne: Melbourne University Publishing.

Marton, Ference, Dai Hounsell and Noel Entwistle. eds. 1997. 2nd edition. *The Experience of Learning: Implications for Teaching and Studying in Higher Education.* Edinburgh: Scottish Academic Press.

Mason, G., G. Williams and S. Cranmer. 2009. 'Employability Skills Initiatives in Higher Education: What Effects do they have on Graduate Labour Market Outcomes?' *Education Economics* 17 1:1–30.

Meyer, Jan H. F., Martin Shanahan and Rüdiger C. Laughksch. 2005. 'Students' Conceptions of Research. 1: A Qualitative and Quantitative Analysis.' *Scandinavian Journal of Educational Research.* 49 3: 225–244 http://users.ugent.be/~mvalcke/CV/conceptions%20of%20research%201.pdf

Moore, Paul and Greg Hampton. 2015. ' "It's a Bit of a Generalisation, but …": Participant Perspectives on Intercultural Group Assessment in Higher Education.' *Assessment & Evaluation in Higher Education* 40 3:390–406. http://dx.doi.org/10.1080/02602938.2014.919437

Morgan, Keith J. 2011. 'Where is von Humboldt's University now?' Research in Higher Education. *Daigaku Ronshu.* 42:325–344 http://rihejoho.hiroshima-u.ac.jp/pdf/ron/42/103772.pdf

Morley, Louise. 2003. *Quality and Power in Higher Education.* Maidenhead: Society for Research into Higher Education and Open University Press.

Mutekwe, Edmore. 2015. 'Towards an African Philosophy of Education for Indigenous Knowledge Systems in Africa.' *Creative Education* 6:1294–1305.

Neary, Mike. 2014. 'From the International Desk: Student as Producer: Research-engaged Teaching Frames University Wide Curriculum Development.' *CUR Quarterly* 35 2:28–34.

Neary, Mike and Joss Winn. 2009. 'The Student as Producer: Reinventing the Student Experience in Higher Education.' In *The Future of Higher Education: Policy, Pedagogy and the Student Experience,* eds. M. Neary, H. Stevenson, and L. Bell, 126–38. London: Continuum. Cited in Levy and Petrulis 2012.

Neumann, Ruth, Sharon Parry and Tony Becher. 2002. 'Teaching and Learning in their Disciplinary Contexts: A Conceptual Analysis.' *Studies in Higher Education* 27 4:405–417. doi: 10.1080/0307507022000011525

Neves, Jonathan. 2016. 'The UK Engagement Survey 2016.' York: Higher Education Academy. https://www.heacademy.ac.uk/uk-engagement-survey-2016-student-engagement-and-skills-development

Nicol, David J. and Debra Macfarlane-Dick. 2006. 'Formative Assessment and Self-regulated Learning: A Model and Seven Principles of Good Feedback Practice.' *Studies in Higher Education* 31 2:199–218. doi: 10.1080/03075070600572090

Nurse, Paul. 2015. 'Ensuring a Successful Research Endeavour.' The Nurse Review of UK Research Councils, Department for Business, Innovation and Skills. BIS/1/624.

Ochsner, Michael, Sven E. Hug and Hans-Dieter Daniel. 2012. 'Four Types of Research in the Humanities: Setting the Stage for Research Quality Criteria in the Humanities.' *Research Evaluation* 2–41. doi:10.1093/reseval/rvs039

Pappas, Stephanie. 2016. 'How Big is the Internet, Really?' *Live Science* 18 March 2016. http://www.livescience.com/54094-how-big-is-the-internet.html

Pinar, William. F. 2012. *What is Curriculum Theory?* 2nd edition. New York: Routledge.

Prosser, Michael and Keith Trigwell. 1999. *Understanding Learning and Teaching: the Experience in Higher Education*. Buckingham: Open University Press.

QAA (Quality Assurance Agency). 2012, September. 'Enterprise and Entrepreneurship Guidance: Guidance for UK Higher Education Providers.' http://www.qaa.ac. uk/publications/information-and-guidance/publication?PubID=70#.WEUlAld_eOo

QAA (Quality Assurance Agency). 2014, June. 'Education for Sustainable Development: Guidance for UK Higher Education Providers.' http://www.qaa.ac.uk/publications/information-and-guidance/publication?PubID=533#.WEUj01d_eOo

QAA (Quality Assurance Agency). 2016a. 'The UK Quality Code for Higher Education: Subject Benchmark Statements.' http://www.qaa.ac.uk/assuring-standards-and-quality/the-quality-code/subject-benchmark-statements

QAA (Quality Assurance Agency). 2016b. Teaching Excellence Framework http://www.qaa.ac.uk/assuring-standards-and-quality/teaching-excellence-framework

Rees, Claire, Peter Forbes and Bianca Kubler. 2007. 2nd revised edition. 'Student Employability Profiles.' York: Higher Education Academy. https://www.heacademy.ac.uk/system/files/student_employability_profiles_apr07.pdf

Reindal, S. M. 2013. '*Bildung*, the Bologna Process and Kierkegaard's Concept of Subjective Thinking.' *Studies in Philosophy and Education* 32:533–549.

Robertson, Jane. 2007. 'Beyond the 'Research/Teaching Nexus': Exploring the Complexity of Academic Experience.' *Studies in Higher Education* 32 5:541–556. Cited in Harland 2016.

Roxå, Torgny and Katarina Mårtensson. 2011. *Understanding Strong Academic Microcultures: An Exploratory Study*. Lund University, April 2011. https://www.lth.se/fileadmin/lth/genombrottet/swednet2011/ReportAcademicMicrocultures.pdf

Schneider, K, 2012. 'The Subject-Object Transformations and *Bildung*.' *Educational Philosophy and Theory* 44 3:302–311.

Shulman, Lee. 2005. 'Signature pedagogies in the professions.' *Daedalus*. Summer 2005. 52–59. http://gse.buffalo.edu/gsefiles/documents/about/Signature-pedagogies-in-the-professions.pdf

Smith, C. 2012. 'Evaluating the Quality of Work-integrated Learning Curricula: A Comprehensive Framework.' *Higher Education Research* & *Development* 31 2:247–262.

Smith, Michelle, Bill Wood, Ken Krauter and Jenny Knight. 2011. 'Combining Peer Discussion with Instructor Explanation Increases Student Learning from In-Class Concept Questions (Molecular, Cellular, & Developmental Biology, CU).' *CBE—Life Sciences Education* 10:55–63.

Snow, C. P. 1959. 'The Two Cultures and the Scientific Revolution.' The Rede Lecture. New York: Cambridge University Press. http://sciencepolicy.colorado.edu/students/envs_5110/snow_1959.pdf

Spencer, David, Matthew Riddle and Bernadette Knewstubb. 2012. 'Curriculum Mapping to Embed Graduate Capabilities.' *Higher Education Research* & *Development* 31 2:217–231. doi:10.1080/07294360.2011.554387

Spronken-Smith, Rachel and Rebecca Walker. 2010. 'Can Inquiry-based Learning Strengthen the Links between Teaching and Disciplinary Research?' *Studies in Higher Education* 35:723–740. doi: 10.1080/03075070903315502

Standen, Alex and Julie Evans. 2015. 'Meet the Researcher: Connecting Students and Researchers from Day One.' Peer-reviewed paper, UK Society for Research into Higher Education Annual Conference, Newport, South Wales. December 2015.

Strom, Margot S. and William S. Parsons. 1994. *Facing History and Ourselves: Holocaust and Human Behavior*. Watertown, MA: Intentional Educations. Cited in Reindal 2013.

Sweeney, Arthur, Scott Weaven and Carmel Herington. 2008. 'Multicultural Influences on Group Learning: A Qualitative Higher Education Study.' *Assessment* & *Evaluation in Higher Education* 33 2:119–132. doi:10.1080/02602930601125665

Tarr, Russel. 2016. 'Ditch Essays for Documentaries.' TES pedagogy. *Times Education Supplement (TES)* 7 October 2016 42–43. https://www.tes.com/news/tes-magazine/tes-magazine/ditch-essays-documentaries

THE (Times Higher Education). 2013. 'V-c: 'Knowledge for Knowledge's Sake' is Piffle.' https://www.timeshighereducation.com/news/v-c-knowledge-for-knowledges-sake-is-piffle/2003445.article

Tong, Vincent, Alex Standen and Asimina Sotiriou. Forthcoming. *Research Equals Teaching: Inspiring Research-based Education through Student-Staff Partnerships*.

Tremblay, K., D. Lalancette and D. Roseveare. 2012. 'Assessment of Higher Education Learning Outcomes AHELO. Feasibility Study.' Volume One: Design and Implementation. OECD http://www.oecd.org/education/skills-beyond-school/AHELOFSReportVolume1.pdf

Tynjälä, P., J. Välimaa and A. Sarja. 2003. 'Pedagogical Perspectives on the Relationships between Higher Education and Working Life.' *Higher Education* 46 2:147–166.

UCISA. 2015. 'Social Media Toolkit: A Practical Guide to Achieving Benefits and Managing Risks.' https://www.ucisa.ac.uk/socialmedia

UCL. 2016a. 'Education Strategy 2016–2021.' https://www.ucl.ac.uk/teaching-learning/2016-21

UCL. 2016b. 'Meet the Researcher': Adaptable Template for Practice. https://www.ucl.ac.uk/teaching-learning/connected-curriculum/Meet_your_researcher

UCL. 2016c. 'Research Excellence Framework (REF) 2014.' https://www.ucl.ac.uk/ref2014

UCL. 2016d. 'UCL 2034: a new 20-year strategy for UCL.' https://www.ucl.ac.uk/2034

UCL. 2016e. UCL Teaching and Learning Portal. https://www.ucl.ac.uk/teaching-learning/

UCL. 2016f. 'Connected Curriculum: Enhancing Programmes of Study.' https://www.ucl.ac.uk/teaching-learning/sites/teaching-learning/files/enhancing_programmes_of_study_sept_2016.pdf

UCL. 2016g. Liberating the Curriculum. https://www.ucl.ac.uk/teaching-learning/education-initiatives/connected-curriculum/liberating-curriculum

UCL. 2016h. UCL ChangeMakers. https://www.ucl.ac.uk/changemakers

UCL. 2016i. UCL Arena. https://www.ucl.ac.uk/teaching-learning/professional-development

UCL. 2016j. R=T (Research equals Teaching). https://www.ucl.ac.uk/teaching-learning/education-initiatives/connected-curriculum/rt-research-teaching

UCL. 2016k. UCL Bachelor of Arts and Sciences (BASc) Programme. https://www.ucl.ac.uk/basc

UCL. 2016m. UCL Integrated Engineering Programme (IEP). http://www.engineering.ucl.ac.uk/integrated-engineering/

UCL. 2016n. UCL Global Citizenship Programme. https://www.ucl.ac.uk/global-citizenship/programme

UCL. 2016o. Introduction to Object-based Learning. http://www.ucl.ac.uk/museums/learning-resources/object-based-learning

UK Commission for Employment and Skills. 2010. 'Employability: Incentivising Improvement.' http://www.educationandemployers.org/wp-content/uploads/2014/06/employability__incentivising_improvement_-_ukces.pdf

UNESCO. 2015. 'Rethinking Education: Towards a Global Common Good?' Paris: United Nations Educational, Scientific and Cultural Organization.

University of Cambridge. 2016. Personal email to the author from Dr Holly Tilbrook, Cambridge Centre for Teaching and Learning, 21 October 2016.

University of Edinburgh. 2016. The University of Edinburgh's Graduate Attributes http://www.ed.ac.uk/employability/graduate-attributes/framework

University of Glasgow. 2016. University of Glasgow Graduate Attributes http://www.gla.ac.uk/media/media_183776_en.pdf

University of Sheffield. 2016. The Sheffield Graduate Attributes https://www.sheffield.ac.uk/sheffieldgraduate/studentattributes

Waghid, Yusef. 2014. *African Philosophy of Education Reconsidered*. Abingdon and New York: Routledge.

Welikala, Thushari. 2011. 'Rethinking Higher Education Curriculum: Mapping the Research Landscape Teaching and Learning.' Position Paper of Universitas 21, August 2011. www.universitas21.com/relatedfile/download/217

Wieman, Carl. 2016a. Carl Wieman Science Education Initiative at the University of British Columbia. http://www.cwsei.ubc.ca/SEI_research/index.html

Wieman, Carl. 2016b. 'A New Model for Post-secondary Education, the Optimized University.' http://www.cwsei.ubc.ca/resources/files/BC_Campus2020_Wieman_think_piece.pdf

Wieman, Carl and Sarah Gilbert. 2015. 'Taking a Scientific Approach to Science Education, Part I—Research and Part II—Changing Teaching.' *Microbe* 10 4:152–156 and 10 5:203–207.

Williams, Peter. 2016. 'Assessing Collaborative Learning: Big Data, Analytics and University Futures.' *Assessment* & *Evaluation in Higher Education.* doi:10.1080/02602938.2016.1216084

Wood, Jamie. 2010. 'Inquiry-based Learning in the Arts: A Meta-analytical Study.' CILASS (Centre for Inquiry-based Learning in the Arts and Social Sciences). University of Sheffield. https://www.sheffield.ac.uk/polopoly_fs/1.122794!/file/IBL_in_Arts-FINAL.pdf

Wray, Mike. 2013. 'Developing an Inclusive Culture in Higher Education: Final Report.' York: Higher Education Academy. https://www.heacademy.ac.uk/system/files/inclusive_culture_report_0.pdf

ndex

Printed in Great
Britain
by Amazon